Christopher Dresser 1834–1904

Michael Whiteway

Christopher Dresser
1834–1904

With a text by Augusto Morello

Scientific Editor
Massimo Valsecchi

Cover
Silver-plate and ebony teapot made by James
Dixon & Sons (see no. 89)

Design
Marcello Francone

Editorial Coordination
Marzia Branca

Editing
Doriana Comerlati

Layout
Paola Ranzini

Translations into English
Language Consulting

Photograph Credits
Photos by Michael Whiteway unless otherwise stated.
Birmingham Library: pp. 163, 167
Chubb Archive, London: pp. 146, 156
The Fine Art Society, London: no. 182; pp. 9, 10, 14
Linnean Society, London: p. 2
Metropolitan Museum of Art, New York: pp. 34-37
Minton Museum & Archives: pp. 26, 32
(2 drawings top left), 50 (centre and bottom),
59 (top right), 67
New Century, London: pp. 33 (top)
Sheffield Archives: pp. 29, 81, 100 (left), 101

First published in Italy in 2001 by
Skira Editore S.p.A.
Palazzo Casati Stampa
via Torino 61
20123 Milano
Italy

© 2001 Michael Whiteway for his texts and the
illustrations
© 2001 Fondazione La Triennale, Milan
© 2001 Skira editore, Milan

All rights reserved under international copyright
conventions.
No part of this book may be reproduced or
utilized in any form or by any means, electronic
or mechanical, including photocopying, recording,
or any information storage and retrieval system,
without permission in writing from the publisher.

Printed and bound in Italy. First edition
ISBN 88-8491-102-8

Distributed in North America and Latin America
by Rizzoli International Publications, Inc. through
St. Martin's Press, 175 Fifth Avenue, New York,
NY 10010.
Distributed elsewhere in the world by Thames
and Hudson Ltd., 181a High Holborn, London
WC1V 7QX, United Kingdom.

This book has been published during the exhibition

"Christopher Dresser. Un designer alla corte della regina Vittoria"

LA TRIENNALE DI MILANO   VENTESIMA ESPOSIZIONE INTERNAZIONALE   2001-2004
XXT La memoria e il futuro

Milan, Palazzo della Triennale
30 October 2001 – 3 March 2002

Exhibition curated by
Massimo Valsecchi, Michael Whiteway

Acknowledgements
This exhibition would not have been possible without the Milan Triennale and its president, Augusto Morello, who had such faith in our project as to make of it the opening event for the 20th international exhibition "La memoria e il futuro", and without the farsightedness and dedication of the lenders who allowed numerous loans from their collections, built up over the last thirty years.
The exhibition is largely made up of four collections, plus very valuable additions from other private collections, museums and institutions.
In thanking these lenders we would like to start with Sophie Cox whose father, the late John Cox, was one of the pioneers in the study of the 19th-century design reform movement. His particular field of interest was metalwork and he gave great encouragement to Michael Whiteway in his early career. John Scott has very generously lent a very large number of exhibits from his extraordinary collection; fortunately these complement the equally generous loans from Andrew McIntosh Patrick and Gilbert & George. Harry Lyons and Dave Bonsall have been very generous with their time, knowledge and loans.
We would also like to thank The British Architectural Library of the Royal Institute of British Architects with Charles W. Hind and Philippa Martin, the South London Gallery with Christopher Jordan, The Fine Art Society, Isabelle Anscombe, Stuart Durant, Sam Fogg, Nancy Glazier, Peter Rose, and the much missed late Albert Gallichan. Joan Jones, curator of the Minton Museum & Archives, Ruth Harman of Sheffield Archives, and David Bishop of Birmingham Library have all made an invaluable contribution. Chris Morley, Stewart Johnson and The Metropolitan Museum of Art, Max Donnelly, Robert Tamakloe, and Neil Phillips have helped with advice and in other ways. Charlotte Gere provided great assistance in reading the text and suggesting improvements. Helen Dunstan, Camellia Stafford, Giovanni Cappelletti, and Roberta Sommariva have helped with numerous problems. Lastly we wish to thank our wives, Mariko and Francesca, for their constant support.
Michael Whiteway, Massimo Valsecchi

Owner credits
The Birkenhead Collection: nos. 1–4, 7, 14–16, 18–22, 25, 27–29, 32–34, 36, 45–49, 51, 52, 85, 98, 118, 120, 128, 129, 139, 140, 142, 144–148, 152, 172, 173, 175, 179, 180, 183, 184, 189, 192, 215–218, 223, 237, 238, 241, 242, 244–246, 248, 251
David Bonsall: nos. 6, 8, 10, 11, 13, 24, 40, 53, 67, 82, 103, 125, 136, 138, 150, 151, 177, 186, 201, 203, 213, 225, 239, 247
The Fine Art Society: nos. 97, 143, 176, 208, 249; pp. 9, 10, 14
Andrew McIntosh Patrick: nos. 39, 41, 54–65, 70, 72–74, 76, 77–79, 83, 84, 86, 89, 90, 94–96, 100, 149, 174, 182, 194, 199, 200, 202, 212, 226
Minton Museum & Archives: pp. 26, 32 (drawings top left), 50 (centre and bottom), 59 (top right), 67
New Century: nos. 12, 74, 87, 91–93, 168, 169–171, 188; pp. 32, 33 (bottom)
Silvia Pearson: nos. 30, 31, 68, 81, 207, 214, 224
Private collections: nos. 5, 9, 17, 23, 26, 35, 38, 39, 42–44, 66, 69, 71, 80, 85, 88, 99, 101, 102, 104–117, 119, 121–124, 126, 127, 130–135, 137, 142, 153–167, 178, 181, 185, 187, 190, 191, 193, 195–198, 204–206, 209, 210, 211, 219–222, 227–236, 240, 243, 250; pp. 30, 31
Sheffield Archives: pp. 29, 81, 100 (left), 101

The British Architectural Library / Royal Institute of British Architects
Nancy Sheiry Glaister Fine and Rare Books
South London Gallery

Contents

8	Introduction *Michael Whiteway*
16	From the Crystal Palace to Christopher Dresser *Augusto Morello*
24	Doctor Christopher Dresser 1834–1904 *Michael Whiteway*
34	The Metropolitan Album
48	Makers that Dresser Designed or Worked for
50	Minton, Stoke on Trent
68	Josiah Wedgwood & Sons, Stoke on Trent
72	Watcombe Terracotta, Torquay
76	Coalbrookdale, Shropshire
80	Dresser's Designs Subsequent to his Visit to Japan
82	Hukin and Heath, Birmingham and London
100	James Dixon & Sons, Sheffield
110	Linthorpe Pottery, Middlesbrough
146	Benham and Froud, London
156	Art Furnishers' Alliance Co., New Bond Street, London
162	Elkington & Co., Birmingham and London
172	Richard Perry, Son & Co., Wolverhampton
176	Old Hall, Hanley
180	Ault, Swadlicote
194	James Couper & Sons, Glasgow
204	Chronology
206	Bibliography

Michael Whiteway

Introduction

The Industrial Revolution had its origins in the eighteenth century, yet the enormous social and structural changes that resulted did not have a great effect until the early nineteenth century. In eighteenth-century England the ideal conditions existed for the Industrial Revolution to take root: scientific ingenuity and entrepreneurial daring met for the first time with a trading infrastructure that provided access to markets. After the Napoleonic wars Britain had no real rivals in Europe, and economic expansion carried on unhindered. This created the conditions and confidence for the investment that was necessary for new technologies to flourish.

One of the most important factors in Britain's industrial superiority was the early development of an effective communications network. The railway system grew rapidly, from 166 miles in 1832 to 6,559 miles in 1850, and, showing unusual foresight, the government legislated to ensure that there was a third class fare affordable to any artisan. The telegraph system soon followed and such was the speed of this new technology that teenage boys were employed as operators. In 1859 Charles Darwin published *The Origin of the Species* changing forever preconceptions of man's place in nature and building one of the most revolutionary of all theoretical constructs – evolution. By 1850 photography had passed from the experimental stage and was becoming a natural way of communicating visual information: for example, John Ruskin, the art critic, employed an assistant to record Venice with daguerreotypes in the 1840s, and the official record of the 1851 Exhibition was illustrated with photographs. In the space of twenty years a revolution in scientific ideas and in communications had taken place. This was a world of unbounded optimism, nevertheless these changes produced inevitable problems.

The growth of the iron, textile and engineering industries meant that vast new conurbations were created to provide labour for the massive new factories.

The urban centres grew so rapidly, that by the 1851 census the urban population actually exceeded the rural. During the nineteenth century, the proportion of the economy derived from agriculture fell from 33% to 7%, at a time when the rest of Europe's population was overwhelmingly rural, and European economies remained largely agrarian.

As many commentators pointed out, there was terrible poverty in these new industrial towns. They had inadequate infrastructures and almost no drainage or proper water supplies. This contributed to regular outbreaks of cholera, and other diseases associated with poverty and overcrowding. A description of Coketown by Charles Dickens: "It was a town of red brick, or of brick that would have been red if the smoke and ashes had allowed it; but, as

Britain in 1850 was supremely self-confident, and this was demonstrated in the bravado with which the scheme for the 1851 Exhibition was conceived. The scale, size, and number of exhibits from all over the world were quite unprecedented, the timescale allowed for this great enterprise being just over one year. Initially it proved impossible to find a satisfactory design for the Exhibition premises, but at a very late stage Joseph Paxton, the eventual architect of the building, heard that there were two more weeks to submit a design. He made his first sketch on a sheet of blotting paper on 11th June 1850 during a business meeting. By the 20th June he had completed detailed plans, and to encourage the committee to decide he published them in the *Illustrated London News* on 6th July. On 15th July Paxton's proposal was accepted, so was the tender for the building work from his collaborators Messrs Fox and Henderson, and they were given possession of the site on the 30th July. By January 1851 the building was completed: a total time from conception to completion of seven months. It was on a grand scale, the main building being three times the length of St Paul's Cathedral: 569 metres long, by 126 metres deep, the maximum height of the transept was 33 metres. There were 13,937 industrial exhibitors, 7,381 from Britain and the empire, and 6,556 from foreign countries, with over 100,000 exhibits. The Exhibition was open for 141 days, and had a total of 6,039,195 visitors (the greatest number was in one day 109,915). The total expenditure (including the cost of the building at approximately £170,000) was £335,742, and the total receipts were £522,179, leaving a profit of £186,437. The industrial age had truly arrived. Without the extensive rail network, the Exhibition could not have existed on this scale, the cast iron components could not have been transported from the Midlands, the public could not have travelled in such numbers to visit. It was also an unprecedented opportunity to compare the products and cultures of the world in one place and represented the beginning of our global culture. Henry Cole, who was one of the main organizers, wrote on the 1851 Exhibition: "The history of the world, I venture to say, records no event comparable in its promotion of human industry, with that of the Great Exhibition of the Works of Industry of All Nations in 1851. A great people invited all civilized nations to a festival, to

Above, previous page and opposite, top: interior and exterior views of the Great Exhibition of the Works of Industry of All Nations, 1851.

matters stood, it was a town of unnatural red and black like the painted face of a savage. It was a town of machinery and tall chimneys, out of which interminable serpents of smoke trailed themselves for ever and ever, and never got uncoiled. It had a black canal in it, and a river that ran purple with ill-smelling dye, and vast piles of buildings full of windows where there was a rattling and a trembling all day long, and where the piston of the steam engine worked monotonously up and down, like the head of an elephant in melancholy madness" (*Hard Times*, 1854).

The Great Exhibition of the Works of Industry of All Nations in 1851 symbolized the full maturity of the Industrial Revolution. To conceive and to construct such a colossal prefabricated iron and glass building, to transport its components via the new railway system, across the country, and to assemble them in the centre of London in Hyde Park, in seven months, showed tremendous confidence in the possibilities of the new industrial and scientific world. It must have seemed possible to build anything. The Great Exhibition attracted over 6 million visitors, had 14,000 exhibitors and over 100,000 exhibits from all over the world. In addition to the industrialized society the Exhibition heralded a new "global economy". For the first time it was possible to witness the diversity of myriad world cultures under one roof. To an impressionable young student, from the schools of design, viewing the magnificent Indian courts, or for that matter the Turkish and Tunisian ones, the world of art must have appeared totally transformed. No longer did it simply consist of the dusty, and much studied cultures of ancient Greece and Rome. However, amidst all this optimism one thing was obvious: design, particularly amongst the British exhibits, was terrible, designers were not exploiting the new industrial processes with any imagination. Throughout the 1840s there had been an awareness of the terrible state of design: the 1851 Exhibition itself was partly the product of these concerns. Prince Albert had actively encouraged the design theorists of this decade, Henry Cole, Owen Jones and others in their struggle to promote a higher standard of design for the Exhibition. The architect A. W. N. Pugin had his own Medieval Court in conjunction with his regular collaborators Minton, Hardman and Crace, but despite all these efforts and concerns the overall standards in the design and execution of the British exhibits remained abysmal. During the 1840s three design theorists had come to prominence.

Firstly, A. W. N. Pugin, who developed many of the principles that were to form the basis of the design reform movement of the latter half of the century: "The two great rules for design are these: 1st, that there should be no features about a building which are not necessary for

Introduction

bring into comparison the works of human skill. It was carried out by its own private means; was self-supporting and independent of taxes and employment of slaves, which great works had exacted in ancient days. A prince of pre-eminent wisdom, of philosophic mind, sagacity, with power of generalship and great practical ability, placed himself at the head of the enterprise, and lead it to triumphant success".

The two greatest engineers of their day, Isambard Kingdom Brunel (*top right*) and Robert Stephenson (*top left*), the year before their death, watching the launching of the *Great Eastern* in 1858. Brunel and Stephenson, together with the steamship's builder John Scott Russell, were officially involved with the Great Exhibition, and Brunel subsequently designed the water towers for the Crystal Palace when it was moved to Sydenham.

Minton tile designed by A. W. N. Pugin decorated using Collins and Reynolds lithographic process, circa 1850. This was a process introduced to Minton by Pugin. Although Pugin publicly despised the world of the Industrial Revolution, he regularly made use of new technologies if they didn't interfere with his ideas. He was one of the first designers to actively seek to exploit industrial processes to realize his designs.

The Crystal Palace at Sydenham. Photo by Philip H. Delamotte, circa 1850. Such was the impact and popularity of Paxton's Crystal Palace building at the 1851 Exhibition that after the end of the exhibition the building was sold for £70,000 to the Crystal Palace Company, and dismantled and re-erected in an enlarged form at Sydenham in south London. It served as an educational display and public resort until it was destroyed by fire in 1936.

convenience, construction or propriety; 2nd, that all ornament should consist of enrichment of the essential construction of the building. The neglect of these two rules is the cause of all the bad architecture of the present time […] the smallest detail should have a meaning or serve a purpose; and even the construction itself should vary with the material employed, and the designs should be adapted to the material in which they are executed" (*The True Principles of Pointed or Christian Architecture*, 1841).

Though he was renowned as a medievalist, Pugin was keen to exploit the new technologies when it suited his purposes: "The steam engine is a most valuable power for sawing, raising, and cleansing stone, timber and other materials. […] It is only when mechanical invention intrudes on the confines of art, and tends to subvert the principles which it would advance, that it becomes objectionable" (*An Apology for the Revival of Christian Architecture in England*, 1843).

Secondly, Owen Jones, who was an ally of Prince Albert, a colour-theorist, the author of the magnificent chromo-lithographic books *Al Hambra*, 1843, and the standard work of reference for future generations of designers – *The Grammar of Ornament*, 1856.

Thirdly, the Victorian critic and connoisseur of art and architecture John Ruskin, author of *The Stones of Venice* 1851 and *The Seven Lamps of Architecture* 1849. Although the three men had little time for each other, they all reached similar conclusions on what constituted good design. They believed in honesty in the choice of materials and the suitability of a design for its function. Each wrote extensively on their ideas, and the next generation of designers absorbed an amalgam of their theories.

The two men largely responsible for organizing the Great Exhibition, Queen Victoria's husband Prince Albert and Henry Cole, also established the Government Schools of Design (1837), and the system of art education, with the specific aim of improving design standards. The South Kensington Museum (later named the Victoria and Albert Museum) was established to provide examples of good design from the past and present for students to study. In 1842 a system of design registration was begun to protect original designs and prevent other manufacturers copying them.

The immense variety and eclectic nature of the goods displayed at the 1851 Exhibition whetted the public's appetite for artistic house decoration, and the next major exhibition in London in 1862 was no disappointment. It was housed in a less radical building, a conventional development of railway architecture combining glass with much brickwork, yet the contents were more sophisticated. A new generation of reforming designers was introduced: the Medieval Court showed

Introduction

The Great Exhibition was not only about consumer goods, it also displayed the altogether more serious side of the Industrial Revolution. Machinery had a much greater impact on the lives of people, as it not only made possible the production of many of the goods on display, but it also helped to create the wealth with which to buy them. Brunel was a member of the machinery section committee, and a judge.

This photo was taken in 1857 at Millwall in East London and shows Brunel's *Great Eastern* being constructed. This was a time of absolute confidence in the possibilities of technology, and the most ambitious projects of the century were happening. Dresser was forming the philosophies that he would adhere to throughout his life. After the excitement of that grandiose feat of engineering, the Crystal Palace, London was soon after treated to another equally ambitious project: the *Great Eastern*. It measured 209 metres and weighted 12,000 tons, several times bigger than any ocean-going ship built previously. Whilst it was being built it achieved such fame that 3,000 tickets were surreptitiously sold for the original and disastrous attempt to launch it. Financially, however, it was a disaster.

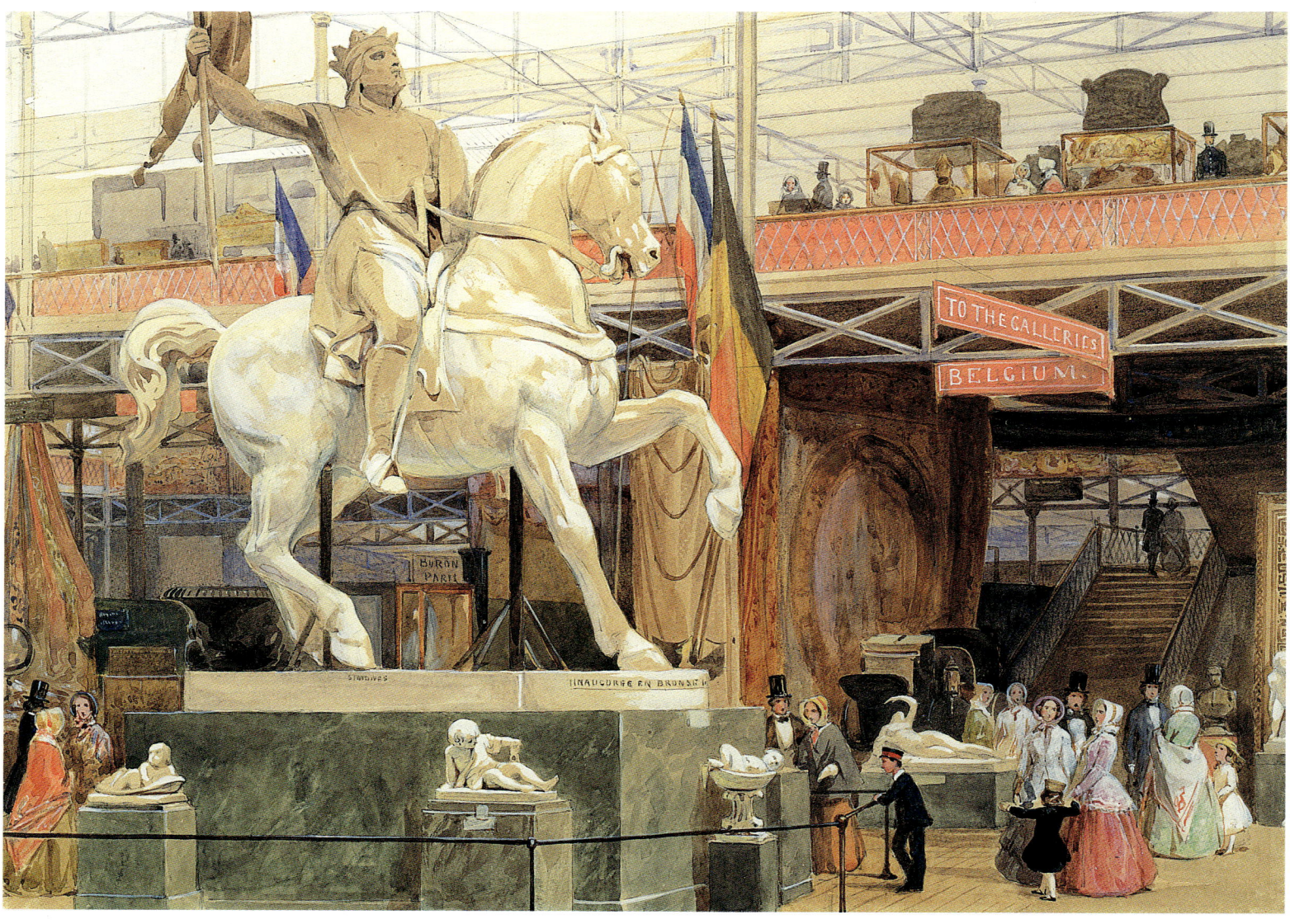

Two views of the London Great Exhibition, 1851.

work by G. E. Street, William Burges, J. P. Seddon, Philip Webb, Richard Norman Shaw, William Morris and Dante Gabriel Rossetti, all of whom could be classed as followers of Pugin and Ruskin. It was here that Christopher Dresser made his debut, exhibiting designs for Minton, the most innovative ceramic manufacturer of the day. Dresser had been a pupil of the South Kensington Schools from 1847. He was a direct product of the new system of art education. Dresser was also a noted botanist and the author of several books on botany, and his scientific training perhaps accounts for the startling originality in his approach to design.

The next major Exhibition was Paris 1867. This Exhibition had many manufacturers employing members of this new design elite to produce enticing new products for the style-conscious industrial middle classes. Most prominent among this new breed of professional designer was Christopher Dresser, who designed products for several exhibiting manufacturers, notably Minton, Coalbrookdale and Wedgwood.

During the next ten years the profession of industrial designer became fully established. New manufacturers of art products appeared, and many new designers came to prominence; the concept

Introduction

of well-designed artistic ornaments for the home became the norm. Among these designers was E. W. Godwin, whose mistress was the most famous actress of the day, Ellen Terry. His circle included James McNeil Whistler and Oscar Wilde. From the 1860s he pioneered the Anglo-Japanese style, designing angular undecorated furniture often consciously intended to be cheap to manufacture.

The hard-won status of the new profession of designer was not to last. A reaction to the Industrial Revolution set in. In 1884 under the influence of William Morris the Art Workers Guild was established, and from that time on the Arts and Crafts movement gained in prestige at the expense of industrial design and the products of the Industrial Revolution. The Arts and Crafts movement espoused the Ruskinian ideals of the dignity of labour, and celebrated the aesthetics of hand craftsmanship to the detriment of machine manufacture and finish. It failed to provide a lasting solution: in reality many of its products were merely amateur and did not answer the everyday needs of the consumer. Unfortunately, the status of designer in Britain was to take half a century to recover.

Augusto Morello — President, Milan Triennale

From the Crystal Palace to Christopher Dresser

Even though quantity and production speed were enormously accelerated, mass production was not peculiar to the Industrial Revolution. Besides, if industrialization were to be understood as mere mass production, it would be only of quantitative value and therefore, even though quantity always seems to "make quality", there would be no justification for using the word "revolution" with which it is so often paired. This raises the question of its causes and its specific methods and effects. Clearly the first developments in industrialization were connected with innovations in energy production, thermal first and then electrical, with performances that rendered energy economically viable by the standards of the day, and with new machines for production (and reproduction) of manufactured articles or parts thereof. Yet it will never be possible to understand the establishment of the industrial method of production without an understanding of the new needs that real demands, even indirectly, conveyed. As there was no private demand for goods that could call for mass production prior to the French Revolution, this demand could only be explained by military, religious, political or other exceptional needs.

A regards military needs, mass production was no novelty, and it was therefore simply a matter of accelerating production mainly by means of mere organization. In the mid-eighteenth century high production rates had been reached even for relatively complex weapons such as the regulation shotgun *Carabina sarda* model 1752, named after the date of its adoption and today housed at Turin Royal Armoury. It was manufactured "at home" in 75,000 copies while 15,000 were commissioned from French producers at Saint-Etienne; a demonstration, moreover, of project transmissibility thanks also to the technical-graphic perfection reached in this period.

Historical documents have shown that this is one of the essential aspects of industrial logic; and it remains today, even with the computer, one of the fundamental conditions not only in project design but also in the passage between project and production. So-called "exceptional" needs (though with time they became less so) were related to the (improper) exportation of metal parts, mostly of agricultural machinery – especially from seafaring nations, Great Britain first and foremost – towards the New World, in aid of the first generations of emigrants, between the end of the sixteenth and the end of the seventeenth centuries.[1] Though it was not difficult to produce wooden parts (such as handles) *in loco*, it was not so easy to manufacture the iron parts. Therefore these were sent to the Americas in great quantity. It was only from the eighteenth century that local production became sufficient to stop the flow from Europe.

Once again it must be pointed out that even before market-pull it is society-push that plays the primary role in spreading innovation; the level of technological complexity is both a motive and effect of innovation itself, including industrialization, which can therefore be considered in itself a meta-innovation. Hence something cannot be defined as industrial (in the modern sense) if its technology is not distinguished by organization, precision, standardization, modularity and not least that it involves a maximum number of equal parts: for all these reasons it can be manufactured by machines which are thus able to produce numerous copies at a time; but it is also necessary to convert the limits of mass production into opportunities. Today all this is called "project management". Industry is therefore a logic system and not simply the production of like objects in quantity.

In the early phases of industrialization goods that already existed were more or less mass produced: invention and innovation – with time always more separate – concentrated on methods and processes of production. Already in 1666 Jean-Baptiste Colbert – Secretary of the French fleet and founder of the East Indies Company – had identified the problem of new techniques at the foundation of the Paris Academy of Sciences, probably in relation to the above-mentioned needs of emigrants (the first permanent French settlement in America was in Michigan in 1641); and in 1695 the Academy decided to set down known techniques meticulously. Later, in 1711, René Antoine Réaumur (1673–1757) – inventor of the alcohol thermometer and the Réaumur temperature scale – was entrusted with the task of compiling a *somme de l'état des arts*. Not "products", it should be pointed out, but "arts", that is to say "organized techniques" for production, quite the contrary of the catalogues produced in the previous century such as that compiled by Jacques Bresson (1578) entitled (and here the different objective is evident) *Théâtre des instruments mathématiques et méchaniques*. Both in Réaumur (which was called *Description des arts et métiers* at its publication in 1757, though issued over a period of thirty years) and in the almost contemporary *Encyclopédie* by Diderot and d'Alembert (1751–72), which was no less rich in commentary and tables (but much more philosophique!), projects for products are presented, but most of all – and in detail – techniques employed. It was a matter of making the results of empirical technical-scientific research accessible to all, thus bringing the culture of technique out of the medieval trade secret mentality, "zeroing" the techniques with the very act of publication. Indeed the mid-eighteenth century could be considered, thanks to these events (even if only on paper), the real beginning of potential industrialization; that is to say, an opening towards widespread innovation.

The next step was taken with the appearance of products that could not have been invented without the knowledge induced from technological research, nor designed with the methods of the seventeenth century, nor could they have been manufactured (technically or economically) without an industrial organizational concept of production. Lynn White, Jr points out that it has become a banality that the most important thing about modern technology is not invention but the "invention of invention".[2]

In actual fact, examining the lists of inventions and innovations it becomes evident that, prior to the *Encyclopédie*, there are no inventions of products that can be authentically defined as "modern" and that are aimed at the final user. It is here that the modern industrial era began; and it was to have its epiphany and its first and greatest public expression in the Great Exhibition of the Works of Industry of All Nations – known as the Great Exhibition – held in London in 1851. And 1851, as will be seen, belonged to the great socio-economic 54-year cycle comprised between 1832 and 1886; yet it was the 1778–1832 cycle that contained the crucial events of the two revolutions, the parallels of which were so skilfully described by Hobsbawm: the French and the Industrial Revolution. The cycle owes its beginning to the protest of Ned Ludd (1779) who, for having smashed a loom, was to give his name to

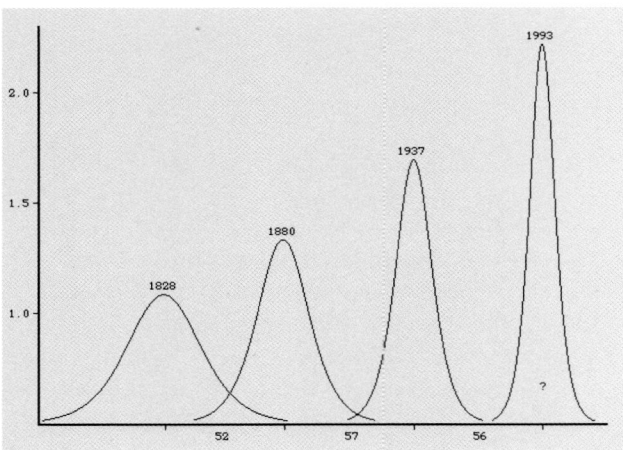

Innovation Waves.
From C. Marchetti, *Society as a Learning System*, IIASA.

the phenomena of Luddism in 1811–16; but it is during the second half of the cycle, around 1805, that the "coexistence" of products manufactured with the new machines and goods – in large or small quantities, especially using moulds or similar methods – that used historically tried and trusted processes became meaningful.

When examining the cultural configuration of product from this period, the influence, and not only in ceramics, of Josiah Wedgwood (1730–1795), who produced high quality ceramics between 1740 and 1760, cannot be overlooked. Among these – alongside the Greek style adapted to the taste of the times – are some forms of innovative freedom.[3]

Likewise the Austrians Michael and August Thonet (1796–1871) from 1821 (and others up to this day) enriched the European production of furniture (especially chairs) made with the new techniques of steam warping beech wood; this developed into true mass production[4] which, much later, was highly praised by Loos, influenced Breuer and was used by Le Corbusier in his interiors. Moreover, because of its quality workmanship, one of the most singular expressions of emigrant material culture in the New World cannot be ignored: that of the Shakers who created, from the last two decades of the eighteenth century (and then, for two hundred years, also using industrial methods), goods of simple structure and purity of line, with catalogues that were widespread even in Europe.

But the most significant event of this period (and not only for its importance to the textile industry) was the invention, in 1801, of Joseph-Marie Jacquard's (1752–1834) automatic loom: the first binary innovation based on the use of perforated cards to produce patterned textiles. The success of Jacquard's loom – a prelude, as we will see, to the modern calculator – was immediate: within ten years there were 11,000 looms operating in France, and the State, fearing that the invention would be exported, "expropriated" the inventor from his patent in exchange for a life income. During the second half of this cycle the architect F. Weinbrenner (1819)[5] had already stated that "beauty lies in the total concordance between form and function". Nonetheless, the production of final user goods was still for the most part characterized by extraneousness of form-configuration from structure, at times from performance and even from cost and the rational of processes; thus widespread conventional formalization was evident.[6]

It can be said then that the theme of industrial design – though yet to be given its modern name – made its appearance well before the macro-economic cycle of 1832–86. But it is only in this cycle that the "possession" of human development by the machine can be recognized, beyond the locomotive (1825–50) and the railway which was the "daughter of the mines" as enthusiastically celebrated as it was feared and abominated. The development of the railway could only have taken place in England, where at the beginning of the nineteenth century they produced 10 million tons of coal a year, that is 90% of world production, though its production of iron was never so significant.[7]

Yet, though the opposition between machine-produced goods and hand-made goods continued through the first half of the cycle, the greater part of products stemming from industrialization and destined for the final user were inventions that had yet to become innovations or were little known.[8]

In *The Great Transformation*, a remarkable book written during World War II, Karl Polanyi (1866–1944) noted that "the nineteenth century was a remarkable phenomenon in the annals of Western history: a hundred years of peace; from 1815 to 1914 [the great powers] were engaged in war for a total of only eighteen months. [In the] two preceding centuries [there had been] an average of sixty or seventy years of significant wars in each century [and] the completely new factor that had emerged was an acute interest in peace".

It was inevitable therefore that, despite the fact that military needs persisted, production turned towards the needs of a prevalently peaceful society.

Nonetheless, quoting Ilbert and Dicey, Polanyi also points out that: "The post-1832 period saw the disorderly construction of an administrative machine of great complexity [in] constant need of repair, renewal, reconstruction and adjustment to new requisites in much the same way as a modern factory"; showing that entrepreneurial organizational ability, and likewise the understanding of the importance of potential demand, had not yet sensitized the awareness of public administration: "l'intendance ne suivait pas".

It is not by chance that – in 1832 – came Nikolaj Kondrat'ev's celebrated periodization which, introduced in 1927 and then studied afresh by Cesare Marchetti,[9] repeatedly captured the attention of a historian of the calibre of Hobsbawm: the century was marked by a socio-cultural cycle that culminated between 1832 and 1886.

1832 was the year of the Reform Act, the birth of the new British Parliament and the Unions for working classes who were humiliated and exploited; but it also marked the intense conversion of invention into that innovation that had been gradually gathering speed over the previous three decades and had reached its climax shortly before, in 1828.[10] By the end of this cycle – around 1886 – the quota of coal had surpassed that of wood (a sign of how things were going in industry), while the rhythm of innovation began to subside, even if Daimler and Benz were successfully experimenting with their motor projects, and Stephenson's rail gauge had been adopted. But 1886 was also the year of Friedrich Nietzsche's *Beyond Good and Evil* and R. L. Stevenson's *Dr. Jekyll and Mr. Hyde*: two titles that can be considered as metaphors of their age.

This period contains practically everything that is included in our survey on memory looking towards the future: the activities of its key players are framed within this fifty-year period, albeit with an appendix that was to lead to the turn of the century. The cycle – as has always happened, at least since then[11] – had a fifteen year incubation period. A real labour market was born in England in 1834 (and therefore, again according to Polanyi, industrial capitalism) with the Poor Law Reform Act; in 1836 the canal infrastructure reached its maximum development, while the railway lines were still growing and were to reach their peak in 1891.[12] 1837 was the year of Charles Dickens' *Pickwick Papers* and *Oliver Twist*, but also the year of Morse's telegraph, and when Queen Victoria ascended the throne (she remained there until 1901); moreover it was the year of Thomas Mann's *Buddenbrooks* and the first electric tram in London. This incubation came to an end around 1846 when the stabilisation phase of the cycle was reached, that is to say the period when science was converted into invention and invention into new artefacts. This period corresponds with Robert Peel's Peel Act, certainly the most important law of the time on industrial finance, but it also corresponded with John Ruskin's *Modern Painters*, the term "folklore" (W. J. Thomas) and the first binary calculating machines, inspired by Jacquard's perforated cards, which Charles Babbage presented in Turin precisely in 1846. As for the matter at hand, in that year A. W. N. Pugin (b. 1812) was 34, John Ruskin (b. 1819) 27, while William Morris and Christopher Dresser (both b. 1834) were little more than 10 years old.

Social and political "response" came immediately: in 1848, the national revolutions, the *Communist Manifesto* the background of which was the utopian Lanark programme (1817) by Robert Owen (1771–1858), but also the foundation of Queen's College, of the Pre-Raphaelite Brotherhood of Burne-Jones, Hunt, Millais, Morris and Rossetti, and Augustus Pugin's project for the catholic cathedral in Southwark. It should be underlined that in 1848, only Britain possessed a real railway network (especially one integrated with the navigation network) which compensated the slowness and inefficiency of the single locomotive: 50% of the capital invested in railways in 1848 was British (according to Cameron). It was only in 1855 that other developed countries ventured to undertake a similar enterprise.

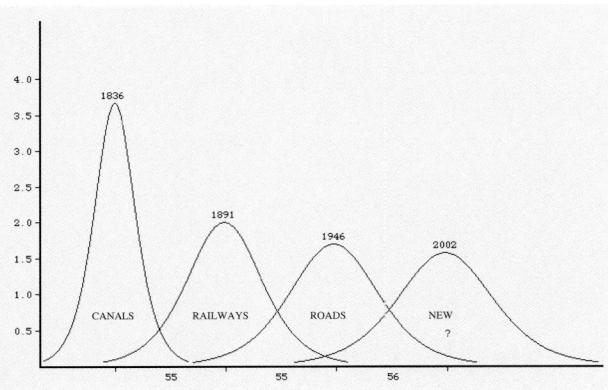

Transport Infrastructures.
From A. Grubler, *The Rise and Fall of Infrastructure*, 1990.

Thus, by 1846–48 the foundations of the transition phase had been laid. But ideas and implementation were not: industry already produced a significant number of products, yet craftsmanship still drew inspiration from the needs of courts, workshop traditions and even peasant working methods; still the greater part of goods were aimed at the aristocracy and upper middle classes. The synthesis by Bertrand Russell[13] regarding the aforementioned text by Owen underlines how forward-looking the prognostication was and therefore how late implementation was to be: Owen "illustrates that the difficulty lies not in producing sufficient quantities but in finding a market. Markets are created by the demand of the working class, which in turn depends on the salaries earned". Indeed the society "that mattered" was torn between good and self-centred intentions, the moralistic concept of charity and the ruthless idea that wealth was the principal proof of quality and therefore almost the only justification for rights. Policies were aimed at efficiency, that is at the relation between results and resource costs; but also determined to increase efficiency by constricting its denominator: Adam Smith had already pointed out that the highest salaries were not to be found in the richest countries. Therefore the recipients could only be the rich, whose financial surplus on possible investments and profits had already reached 60 million pounds by 1840 (Hobsbawm).

But, despite all of this, a new social class of specialized craftsmen, white collars, small traders began to have some weight in matters of demand, both utilitarian and artistic; the latter provided items for just a few pounds that were not so atrocious. John E. Millais and his associates were soon to make a fortune with works costing two guineas a piece.[14]

In 1840 Queen Victoria, at the age of twenty-one, married Albert of Saxe-Coburg-Gotha,(1819–1861) who was her same age. Somewhat pompous, his contemporaries considered him to be melancholic, pedantic with his children, puritanical and stubborn, tight-fisted and not without psychological disorders; he had difficulty in learning the English language, though he admired English literature along with mathematics, philosophy and political science, also spurred by a certain amount of conceit. Yet, despite the fact that his German origins may have influenced the opinion of many British observers, he was the only member of the English court who attempted to open relations with cultural environments that were more advanced than those that generally attended the insipid Victorian court: in just over twenty years of their marriage Albert was the intellectual shadow of a queen that history has irredeemably judged as superficial and conformist. He quickly showed an extraordinary interest in the economic aspects of artistic issues, at least when compared to his *milieu*.

The *Art Union* had appeared in London in 1839 (S. Carter Hall, 1800–1899), which, renamed the *Art Journal* after 1839, was published under the patronage of the prince from 1847 and published the catalogue of the Great Exhibition. This was also thanks to the intervention of Sir Henry Cole (1808–1882), the pedagogue who founded the *Journal of Design and Manufacture* (1849) considered the first review of design, on whose advice the exhibition was held and who coined the expression "art manufacturer". A series of exhibitions had been held in France since 1798: the most important were the Expositions Industrielles in 1844 and 1849. The British government ignored all suggestions to follow the French example, and the only exhibition held in Great Britain was on metal products in 1849 in Birmingham. Albert's intervention was decisive for an exposition on the "works of world industry" that was to be held in 1851. Thus the prince obtained the nomination of a Royal Commission from the government after a speech describing the event as one that "would afford a true test of the point of development at which the whole of mankind has arrived in this great task, and a new starting point from which all nations would be able to direct their further exertions".

The commission met in January 1850 and the mayors of the entire country were invited to a sumptuous banquet at the Mansion House. On that occasion the prince gave another important speech, with the result that 230,000 pounds were collected – which, considering the surplus mentioned above, was not a difficult sum to obtain – for an exposition that would be greater than any ever held in France. A competition was organized in which 38 foreign architects took part alongside 128 from London alone and 51 from the rest of Great Britain; but no single project was deemed to respond to the briefing. Therefore the commission adopted a project of their own, provoking the protests of the competitors; the contractor presented an estimate for the project, but this had been revised to the point of having little to do with the original. The new project was based on a plan by Joseph Paxton (1803–1865) that had simply been sketched on a piece of blotting paper. Paxton, who was assistant gardener and later designer of a glasshouse for the Duke of Devonshire, was requested to present the completed project within nine days. The final project was presented on 22nd June 1850 and published in the *Illustrated London News* on 6th July. But serious doubts regarding the stability and safety of the building were raised by the royal astronomer Airey and by Turner, who had already built the Palm House in Kew Gardens; they warned of the risk of a collapse caused by dangerous vibrations due to the movements of the large crowds expected: the phenomenon was known in bridges on which soldiers should not march in step. Thus a construction test was carried out with 300 workers and soldiers who walked back and forth both in step and normally and even jumping all together; the maximum movement observed was of a quarter of an inch and so the enormous building went ahead. 772,784 square feet (19 acres) indoors, as well as 217,100 square feet of galleries: an area that was four times the size of Saint Peter's in Rome, six times that of Saint Paul's in London and three times as high. These the antecedents and the history of the pragmatism of the Great Exhibition at Hyde Park for which in 1851 – not by chance the year that the Reuter Agency was founded, and just after the death of Robert Peel, the year of the first novel on conditions in the industrial era (Ch. Kingsley, *Alton Locke*), of the first petrol refinement and but a few years after the appearance of the word "modern" – Albert had decided and Paxton had built – thirty-eight years before the Eiffel Tower (1889) – the great modular and prefabricated Crystal Palace.

On 1st May 1851 the Exhibition was inaugurated in the presence of Victoria and Albert, 300,000 guests and 700,000 onlookers – but the kings of Europe were absent. With 14,000 exhibitors and 6 million visitors at the end of the Exhibition on 11th October 1851 Albert had made a profit of about 186,000 pounds, later used to build the Victoria and Albert Museum. In a United Kingdom that had, at that time, a population of less than 30 million inhabitants, this number cannot but be amazing without even considering the number of foreign visitors. The earnings included 40,000 pounds from ticket sales, 3,200 pounds for the honour of printing the catalogues and 5,500 for the privilege of supplying refreshments. After the Great Exposition the Crystal Palace was reconstructed at Sydenham under the supervision of Paxton and was open to the public until its destruction by fire in 1936. Nonetheless the park at Sydenham is still known as Crystal Palace. The London event was followed four years later by exhibitions in Paris (24,000 expositors), in 1859 in Turin and yet another in London in 1862 (29,000 expositors), again in Paris in 1867 (50,000 expositors) and still other expositions elsewhere, always with an attendance between 5 and 9 million visitors. At these exhibitions thousands of products were presented; the greater part were pre-industrial goods in serial format: but the great value of these reviews – from the very first – lies in having presented the products of the time all together, which, as they were prevalently industrial, sensitized distribution to the concept of "variety" (in those years the idea of "organized distribution" was born), favouring competition both for the good it brought to supply and the equality it brought to demand.

But the opinion of many writers was that the aesthetic quality continued to be poor,

[1] The earliest European landings in North America included one in 1584 by the British at Roanoke Island, North Carolina, and one in 1562 by the French at a site they called Charlesfort. The most famous settlement is of course the one in Virginia in 1607, which has been called the birthplace of America (and it was the setting for the Pocahontas story, now proven to be substantially true). The hundred colonists were poorly outfitted, with muskets dating from a century earlier, and relied on very primitive technologies. After a year, only thirty-eight remained.
[2] Lynn White jr, *Medieval Technology and Social Change*, Oxford, 1962.
[3] There are, for example, some fine ceramics dated 1760 at the Victoria and Albert Museum.
[4] In 1876 Thonet had 4,500 employees, 10 steam-warping machines and 280 horses installed, and produced 2,000 items per day, 80% of which were chairs. By 1900 daily production, in 26 factories, had risen to 15,000 units.
[5] Noted by Tomás Maldonado in his short but precious *Disegno industriale: un riesame*, taken from the entry in the *Enciclopedia Treccani del Novecento*, 1976, later integrated in 1991.
[6] It is worth mentioning Watt's steam engine (1777), the mechanical spinning machine and the first iron bridge (1779), the steamship (1783), Cartwright's mechanical loom (1785), Jacquard's loom (1801), the industrial production of paper (1807), and the industrial sewing machine (1830). The first products produced on an industrial scale for the end user were concentrated in the second half of the cycle with gas street lighting (1807), Pellegrino Turri's

certainly far from that hoped for by Weinbrenner in the quotation above. Indeed, there had been an imposing quantity of industrial variants on products that were not new – for which it was claimed (differently from today) that the quality of machine-made products could only but be better than those made by hand thanks to the infallibility of the machine: labels were even put on the products ("completely machine-made") – and a much smaller number of basic phenotypes for new genotypes. It seemed that awareness continued to be lacking of possible new configurations within machine production. It has also been suggested that this awareness was to be prompted precisely by the mass of inadequate projects that the great Exhibitions, especially at London, had made simultaneously visible: in this sense (but only in this sense) the London Exhibition can be considered – after a century – the epiphany of the enlightenment's *Encyclopédie*. Who does not remember the anti-industrial position of William Morris, alongside his talent as a decorator, and graphic and furniture designer? At the time of the Great Exhibition he was but 17 years old, as was Christopher Dresser; but both were 28 at the following Exhibition. Morris, also influenced by the art critic John Ruskin, was a strenuous supporter of manual production and the direct relationship between man and his manufacture: even when working (as he himself did) with machines, or when his designs had to be entrusted to others, and consequently deprived of any intellectual participation. The difference in reaction between Morris and Dresser to the inadequacies seen in the London Exhibitions – and the latter was to work until the take-off of the successive cycle – puts Christopher Dresser, probably, in the position of being the world's first modern industrial designer.

Our aim here has been to illustrate this extraordinary social transition to industrial design, drawing out for comparison the attitudes – however unconscious – of the most celebrated exponents of Arts & Crafts, and the partiality of what has been written to date regarding their exquisite elegance. It should always be remembered – especially in today's design crisis – how the makings and doings of the future cannot be separated from the choices of memory.

---

typewriter (1808), canned food (1811), miners' lamps (1815), and bicycles (1816).
[7] Cf. Eric J. Hobsbawm, *The Age of Revolution: Europe 1789-1848*, New York, 1969.
[8] We can cite as examples for the first part of the cycle: the daguerreotype and air-conditioning (1837), the pedal bicycle (1838), gas cookers for restaurants and electroplating (1839), the stamp, the photographic lens and metal tubes for paints (1840), adhesive envelopes and inflatable lifejackets (1844), pneumatic tyres (1845), the sewing machine (1845-51), nitro-glycerine (1846), the clockwork toy train (1856), the elevator and electric street lighting (1857), the refrigerator, condensed milk, colour printing, the family sewing machine and the first ship with a metal body for 4,000 passengers (1858), the storage battery and Pacinotti's ring (1859).
[9] Cf. C. Marchetti, *Society as a Learning System*, IIASA papers, 1978.
[10] See diagram p. 18.
[11] A 54-year cycle is governed by a symmetric logic or an S-shaped curve (called "Volterra-Lotka curve") applicable to various factors of the cycle itself. Halfway through the cycle the curve, previously in continuous growth, begins to slow towards a *plafond* after which another cycle begins. While in the central twenty-seven years the curve is usually well defined, in the first and last quarters (thirteen-fourteen years, which correspond to 10% and 90% of development) it is more disturbed. The first of these quarters can be defined as the "take-off" and at its conclusion the dynamic profile of the cycle can be considered stabilized.
[12] See diagram p. 20.
[13] Cf. *Freedom and Organisation*, London, 1934.
[14] Cf. G. Reitlinger, *The Economics of Taste*, London, 1961; quoted by Hobsbawm, *The Age of Capital*, New York, 1975.

Michael Whiteway

Dr Christopher Dresser 1834–1904

Christopher Dresser was born in Glasgow in 1834, the same year as William Morris. Unlike Morris who came from a very prosperous family, Dresser's background was modest: his father was a tax collector and was regularly posted to different areas; five years of Dresser's childhood were spent in Ireland. He was an artistic child and possessed an extraordinary talent. Because of this, in 1847 he was admitted at the age of thirteen – two years earlier than usual – to the newly formed Government Schools of Design. As well as studying art, the young Christopher Dresser studied botany, publishing three books during the 1850s and receiving a doctorate in botany from Jena University, in Germany.

In 1860 Dresser failed to obtain the chair of Botany at London University and from this point on appears to have concentrated on the more lucrative field of design. It is important to note, however, that in the mid-nineteenth century the disciplines of design and botany covered much common ground. Dresser was, after all, educated at the Schools of Design, where pupils were presented weekly with examples of flora and fauna from the gardens at Kew to analyse in their studies. Dresser rapidly established himself as a very successful practitioner. In 1862 he published his first two books on the theory of design, *The Art of Decorative Design*, and *Development of Ornamental Art at the International Exhibition*, the latter referring to the 1862 Exhibition in London. Dresser designed ceramics for Minton which were on show at the exhibition, and purchased some of the items of Japanese art from the collection of Sir Rutherford Alcock. This was the first time that Japanese art had been shown publicly in Britain. The 1862 Exhibition also marked the public debut of William Morris and his circle, as well as other stars of the future such as Richard Norman Shaw and William Burges. Manufacturers such as Templetons showed well-designed art objects, a contrast to 1851 when almost no objects of merit were exhibited, with the exception of the works in Pugin's renowned Medieval Court.

Throughout the 1860s and 1870s Dresser seems to have thrived. He maintained a design studio employing many designers (one of these was J. Moyr Smith who was to become renowned in his own right), and developed a house style based on his highly original design theories. According to Nicholas Pevsner, who wrote the first modern article on Dresser in 1937, based on interviews with his daughters, in 1869 he supplied 158 sketches for silk damasks to Wards of Halifax, and 67 sketches of carpets to Brintons as well as many designs to other manufactures. In 1871 he provided 142 carpet designs to the manufacturer John Crossley & Sons. By 1868 Dresser was prosperous enough to move to a large house in a prestigious part of London, Tower Cressy in Aubrey Road,

Dr Christopher Dresser 1834–1904

Plate XCVII from *The Grammar of Ornament* by Owen Jones, 1856. This is the only plate in this highly influential book drawn by Dresser. Throughout his career Dresser acknowledged Jones's influence on him, and when he was appointed editor of the *Furniture Gazette* he adopted Jones's "principles" as those of the magazine. Whilst at the Government Schools of Design, one of Dresser's disciplines was to study botany, in which he excelled. He published three books on the subject, and in 1860 Jena University awarded him a doctorate in botany. Dresser's botanical studies were to play an important part in his philosophy as a designer. His observations on the adaptability of plants to their environment influenced his approach to materials, and his theories on the innate symmetry of plant forms helped him develop a structure in his designs.

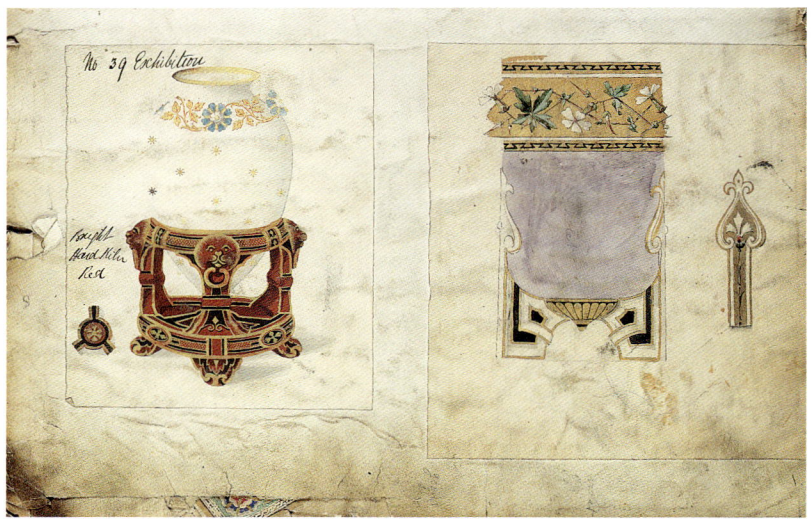

Design for a vase made by Minton and shown at the 1862 International Exhibition in London. This was the first time that Dresser had his designs displayed in front of an international audience.

Campden Hill, and he ran his studio from this address.

Instead of concerning himself as most Victorian architects did with the battle of the styles, Gothic versus Classical, Dresser followed his mentor Owen Jones in his admiration for Oriental art. Based on his observations as a scientist and his study of art from the Orient, Dresser strove to invent a truly modern style. The status which he accorded to ornament can be gathered from a paper which he gave to the Royal Society of Arts in 1871: "True ornamentation is of purely mental origin, and consists of symbolized imagination or emotion only. I therefore argue that ornamentation is not only fine art, but that it is high art […] even a higher art than that practised by the pictorial artist, as it is of wholly mental origin". During the 1860s and 1870s, apart from his few designs for Minton, Coalbrookdale, Wedgwood and others, the great majority of Dresser's studio output had been for ornament: carpet, wallpaper and textile designs. These were industries of vast size and variety, and economically far more important than the pottery and silver businesses. He claimed in 1871: "As an ornamentist I have much the largest practice in the kingdom; so far as I know, there is not one branch of art-manufacture that I do not regularly design patterns for, and I hold regular appointments as 'art-adviser' and 'chief-designer' to several of our largest art-manufacturing firms".

Unfortunately, textiles and wallpaper are perishable and transitory, and very little of Dresser's vast output has survived. The design book we illustrate dates from the 1880s, but includes designs for patterns from throughout Dresser's career, and it gives some idea of the range of his production. It is important to emphasize that he maintained a large studio and that not every design even in this book is necessarily completely by his hand, even though it bears his name, but all have been endorsed by him and have come from his studio.

In 1876 Dresser sailed from Liverpool on the first stage of what would be the most important journey of his career, his journey to Japan. Japan and its art had become increasingly fashionable amongst certain avant-garde circles. Of Dresser's contemporaries, the best known group of such enthusiasts was the circle of Oscar Wilde, Whistler and their architect E. W. Godwin. The latter pioneered the design of geometric and unadorned furniture, advocating plain interior decoration, exemplified in the treatment of his own home, decorated in shades of grey. Dresser's first stop was America, where he visited the 1876 Philadelphia Centennial Exhibition. Whilst he was there he sold designs to several local manufacturers, and was appointed as a buyer by Tiffany & Co. of New York. Then he travelled by rail to San Francisco, and from there set sail to his final destination, Japan.

He visited Japan in a semi-official capacity, he brought examples of British manufacture as gifts for the National Museum, and he also had the rare privilege of being presented to the emperor. At this stage Japan was not yet fully accessible and Dresser saw areas from which other Westerners were excluded. Although the country was rapidly changing, Dresser was still able to experience traditional Japan; indeed, the Satsuma rebellion, the last stand of traditional samurai life, was occurring whilst he was there and prevented him from visiting one of the main centres of the ceramics industry. Dresser used his visit to undertake a comprehensive study of Japanese art. During his four-month-long stay he visited 68 potteries, 100 temples and had more than 1,000 photographs taken.

On his return to England Dresser's work underwent a profound and fundamental change.

Although his studio probably carried on much as before designing ornament, Dresser himself embarked on a series of radically different designs. In 1878 he completed a series of original and startling designs in silver and electroplate for Hukin and Heath, a firm who specialized in novelty ware, supplying shops in the West End of London. These designs were almost totally devoid of ornament, and relied on form for their impact. Where examples were made in silver the design would recognize this and use the material

Cover of *The Art of Decorative Design* and page with the motto "Knowledge is Power". Published in 1862, it was the first of Dresser's books on design theory, which publicized him as a designer and set out the principles on which he was to base the development of his ideas on design.

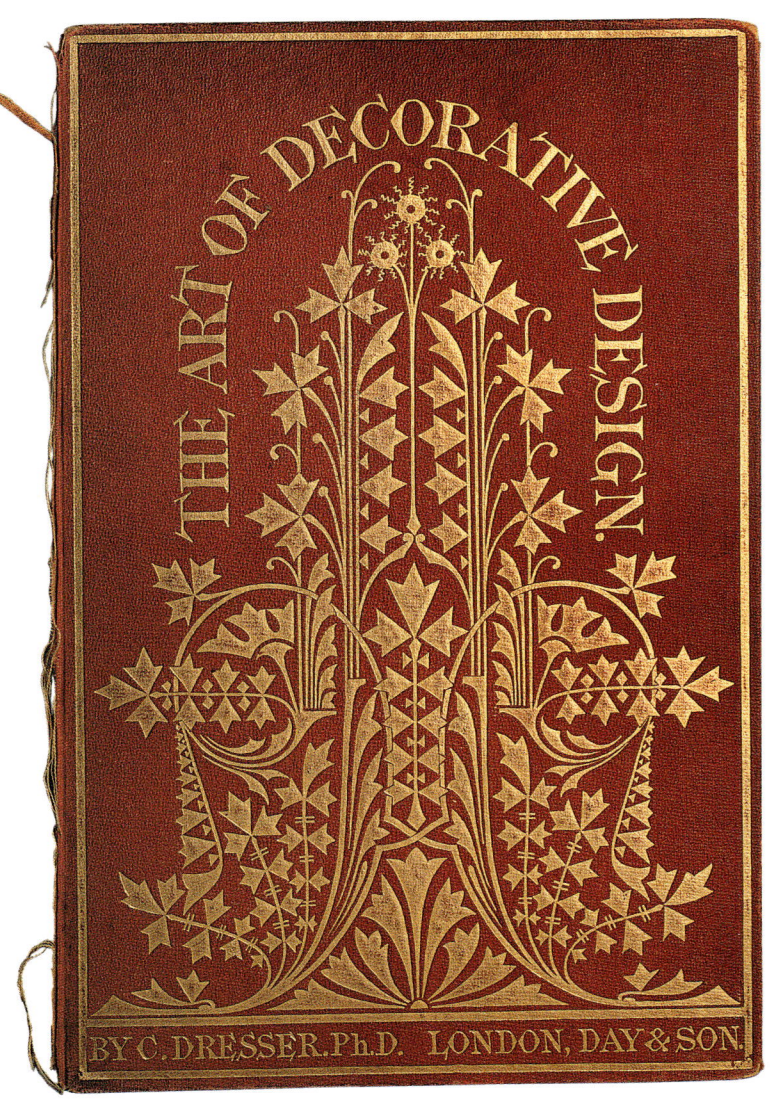

Conceived in what Dresser describes as a moment of true inspiration, this design from his most lavish book, Studies in Design, was based on sketches made in 1856 of frost on his window. He did not develop these ideas for a further eight years.
Dresser sought to raise the status of ornament and in 1871 he said before an audience at the Royal Society of Arts: "True ornamentation is of purely mental origin, and consists of symbolized imagination only. […] Ornamentation is […] even a higher art than that practised by the pictorial artist, as it is of wholly mental origin".

economically. Hukin and Heath held a sensational exhibition of these designs at their new premises at 19 Charterhouse Street in August 1879. In the same year Dresser was also instrumental in the founding of an ambitious enterprise: Linthorpe Art Pottery, financed by the entrepreneur John Harrison in Middlesbrough to be an art complex. Dresser was the art director, and in the event only art pottery was produced. Linthorpe pottery was like nothing that had preceded it, it was inspired by Dresser's observations of Japanese pottery, exploiting the plasticity of clay. Linthorpe shapes were suited to their medium and did not try to imitate metal or stone. Abstract dribbling glazes that relied on chance for their effects supplied the ornament. This was like nothing that had been seen before in Western ceramics.
1879 also saw Dresser producing an even more avant-garde group of designs for another manufacturer of electroplated wares, James Dixon & Sons. A feature of all these designs produced after Dresser's journey to Japan is that the actual objects are marked with his name, either in the form of a facsimile signature, or of the inscription "Dr Dresser's Design". The concept of actually crediting a designer's name on an object was unprecedented, and indicates the level of Dresser's prestige.
In 1880 Dresser embarked on the inevitable culmination of all his experimentation in aesthetics: he established in Bond Street, in the West End of London, a store for the admirer of advanced taste, the Art Furnishers' Alliance. The prospectus said it had been formed "for the purpose of supplying all kinds of house-furnishing material, including furniture, carpets, wall-decorations, hangings, pottery, table-glass, silversmiths' wares, hardware, and whatever is necessary to our household requirements […] the art direction of the new warehouse will be left in the hands of Dr Christopher Dresser, FLS etc., who will be the art authority of the company, and no object, whether an important work or a mere adjunct of furnishing, will be offered for sale in the Companies warehouse unless he testifies of its art qualities".
The Art Furnishers' Alliance had as suppliers of Oriental art Arthur Lazenby Liberty and Dresser and Holme, they stocked metalwork to Dresser's design made by Hukin and Heath, James Dixon & Sons, and Benham and Froud, pottery by Linthorpe, and wallpapers by five different makers. Unfortunately the Art Furnishers' Alliance was not a financial success, and in 1883 it went into liquidation.
From this time on Dresser's fortunes declined, he moved from his central London house to a distant suburb, and although he still produced some remarkable work, notably for Elkingtons and Clutha, he never achieved the same level of fame again. Not only did he suffer financially, but also fashions were changing, and many of his contemporaries died around this time: Bruce Talbert and William Burges in 1881, and E. W. Godwin in 1886. Apart from Dresser, the most prominent designer of the applied arts who remained was William Morris. Morris was instrumental in the foundation of the Art Workers Guild in 1884, which included among its members many architects of the younger generation. The Arts and Crafts movement was rapidly usurping Dresser's role and his ideas as a designer. From this time on, his exact contemporary William Morris would achieve such fame that it would seem that he alone was responsible for the revolution in design that occurred in England during the nineteenth century.

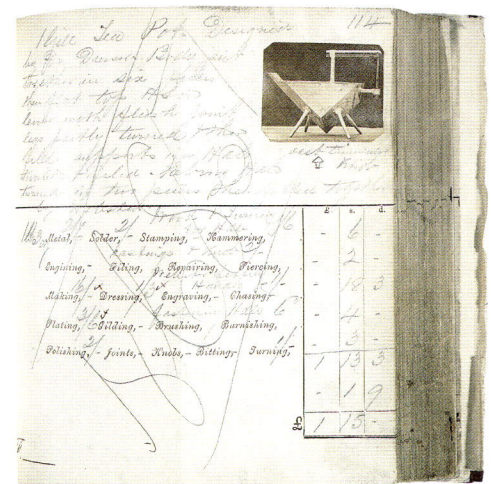
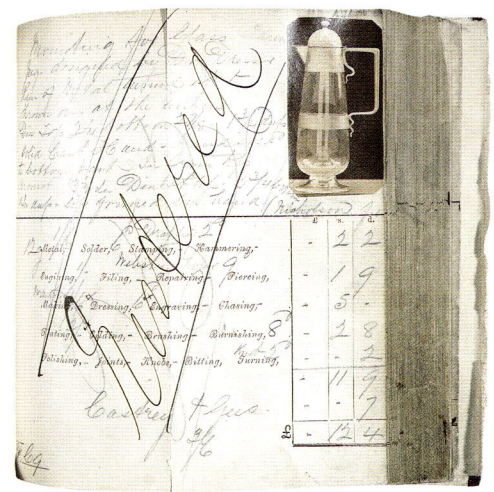
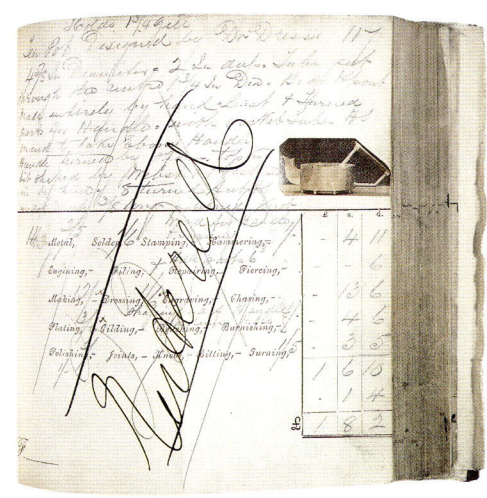

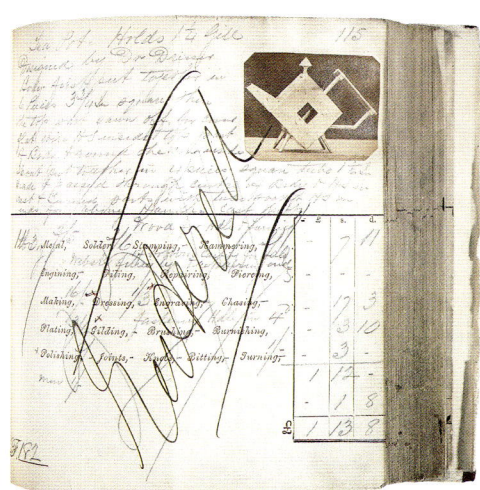
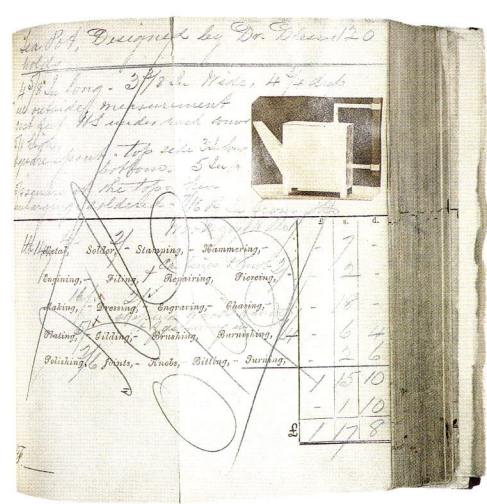
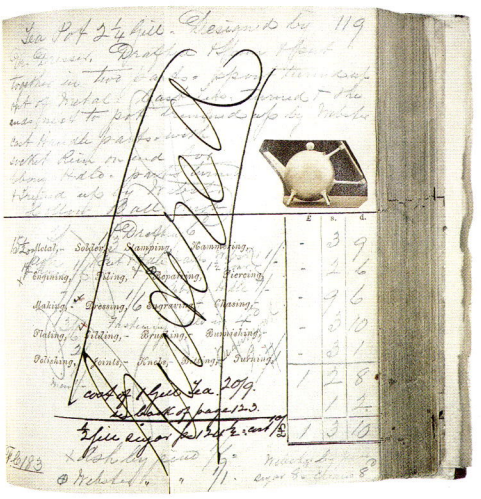
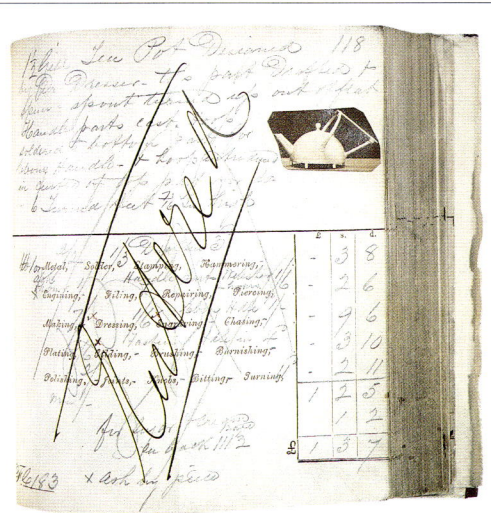

Eight pages from James Dixon & Sons 1879 cost book showing Dresser's designs.

These contemporary photographs of James Dixon & Sons products illustrate just how different Dresser's designs were to those normally offered to the public, forgoing the customary surface decoration of conventional Victorian design, and relying instead on form for visual impact. Most of the designs illustrated must have been made in very small quantities as only a few of them have survived.

Table designed by E. W. Godwin and made by Collinson and Lock, circa 1874. The Metropolitan Museum of Art, New York. There were other designers apart from Dresser who had both the enthusiasm for and the understanding of Japanese art that was necessary to assimilate its basic principles. Godwin collaborated with the painter James McNeil Whistler at the 1878 Paris Exhibition, on the stand of the furniture maker William Watt. Godwin also designed Whistler's studio: the White House in Tite Street, Chelsea, London; this house was almost totally without historical reference, relying on colour and the asymmetric layout of the façade for visual effect.

Sake bottle made by Linthorpe, circa 1880 (see no. 162). When Dresser visited Japan he would have seen much domestic pottery. The Japanese pottery familiar to Westerners was very different to wares that the Japanese themselves used, as it was produced to satisfy Western tastes. "When I started for Japan I thought my knowledge of Japanese potteries and pots tolerably perfect; but when I returned from that country, after visiting nearly 70 potteries, I came to the conclusion that even my knowledge of Japanese ceramics was most limited." On Dresser's return to England, his designs for ceramics changed fundamentally. Inspired by the Japanese exploitation of the plasticity and malleability of clay, he rejected the European tradition of making clay imitate metallic or sculptural forms, and designed a series of designs for the Linthorpe pottery utilizing the natural properties of the material.

Dr Christopher Dresser 1834–1904

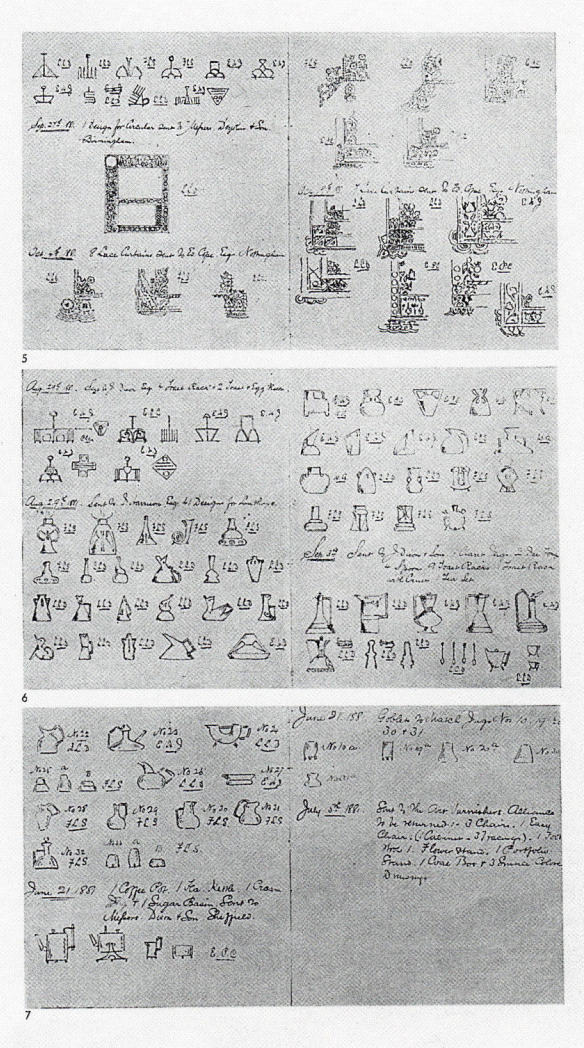

Three pages of designs from Dresser's 1881 account book. The architectural historian Nicholas Pevsner wrote a pioneering article on Christopher Dresser in 1937 in the *Architectural Review*, based on interviews with his daughters. He illustrated these sketches from Dresser's 1881 account book, which show designs supplied to James Dixon & Sons, the Linthorpe Art Pottery and the Art Furnishers' Alliance. He describes the scale of his business: for instance, in 1869 he supplied 158 sketches to Wards of Halifax, and 67 carpet designs to Brintons as well as many other designs to other manufactures. Minton paid Dresser the sum of £4.10 for a design for a cup and saucer, and £10.50 for a large vase, for carpets he was paid between £3.15 and £10.50 and for textile designs between £10.50 and £21.

Silver jug by Tiffany and Co., circa 1880. Throughout his career, Dresser not only worked as a designer, but also as an advisor and in the case of Tiffany and Co. an agent. When Dresser visited Japan in 1877 one of his roles was as a buyer for Tiffany and Co., and in his book *Japan. Its Architecture, Art and Art Manufactures*, published in 1882 he observes: "I certainly had the honour of being entrusted by Messrs Tiffany & Co. with the choice of any objects that I might think calculated to aid in their silversmith business; and it is interesting to me to know that, after a most careful and intelligent consideration of these objects, Messrs Tiffany & Co. produced new works which produced to the firm the 'Grand Prix' at the last Paris Exhibition". It is also tempting to speculate whether Dresser's Clutha glass of 1888 had any influence on Louis C. Tiffany's Favrile glass.

Above, left: two designs for Minton by Christopher Dresser, circa 1860–70. *Above, right*: page from Pugin's *Floriated Ornament*, 1849. Dresser was part of the second wave of the design reform movement, and as can be seen in the similarity of these two designs, he owed a debt to the pioneers of the previous generation, and particularly A. W. N. Pugin. Pugin had been in many ways the pioneer of industrial design in England; he designed ceramics for Minton, carpets, wallpapers, furniture and metalwork, and wherever it was expedient he utilised the latest technologies. One major difference between Pugin and Dresser was that most of Pugin's designs were originally commissioned for architectural schemes, whereas Dresser intentionally designed objects for retail sale.

Detail of a cruet by Hukin and Heath showing the registration mark together with "Designed by Dr C. Dresser". In 1842 the government set up a system of design registration to protect designs from plagiarism. Dresser was the only designer to apply his name to products for different manufacturers; this symbol of authenticity reassured customers that their taste must be impeccable.

32

Dr Christopher Dresser 1834–1904

Detail of ceiling decoration for Allangate, Halifax, built for Thomas Shaw, 1869–70. Dresser decorated Allangate at the height of his success as an "ornamentist". This is one of only two schemes that survive, and can be compared with Owen Jones's scheme for Alfred Morrison at Carlton House Terrace in London.

Woven wool and silk textile made by W & C Ward, 1871. Throughout his career most of Dresser's production was for ornament. Due to the transitory nature of textiles, wallpapers and carpets, not much has survived except for fragments in archives.

1860–1880
The Metropolitan Album

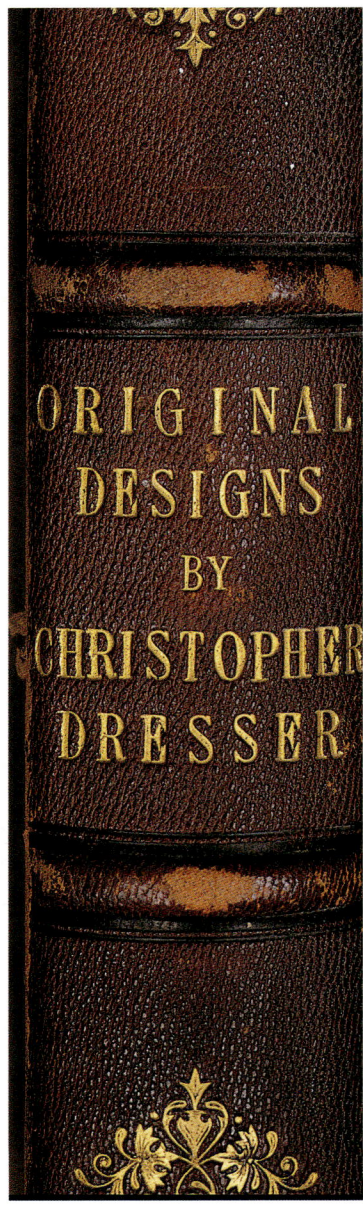

This album (The Metropolitan Museum of Art, New York) is inscribed by Dresser, and dates from the period in the 1880s when his career was at its lowest ebb. Dresser had moved from his London house to the suburb of Sutton, after the collapse of the Art Furnishers' Alliance. The album appears to be a sample book, and shows the range of his designs. The contents date from throughout his career; the earliest designs including his *Frost* stained glass window and his *Band of Brothers* for Minton date from about 1870, and the latest from the mid-1880s. They give a good idea of his range of designs for ornament. It is interesting to note that Dresser was still showing designs that were nearly twenty years old to prospective customers in the 1880s.

The Metropolitan Album 1860–1880

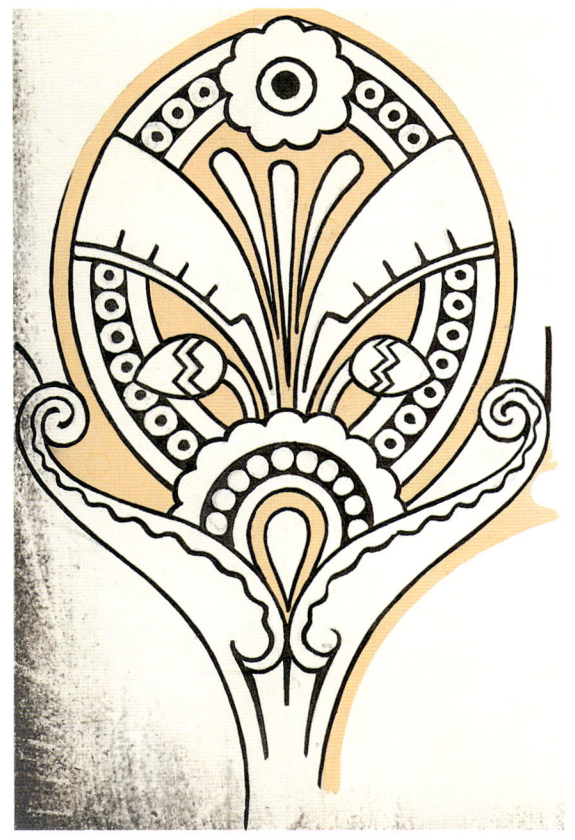

The Metropolitan Album 1860–1880

The Metropolitan Album 1860–1880

The Metropolitan Album 1860–1880

Makers that Dresser Designed or Worked for

Christopher Dresser had been a pupil at the Government Schools of Design from 1847, and was therefore a direct product of the new system of art education. Whilst a student he would have absorbed the current theories on design reform as expounded by A. W. N. Pugin, Owen Jones, John Ruskin and other design reformers. Dresser was also a noted botanist and author of several books on the subject; perhaps the fact that he received a scientific training accounts for the startling originality in his approach to design.

Throughout his career Dresser seems to have taken great care in choosing the type of manufacturer with whom he wished to collaborate. Mostly they were leaders in the exploitation of the technology of the day: the Coalbrookdale cast iron works, the pioneer of electroplating Elkington, or the ceramic manufacturers Minton. Dresser was their ideal partner, as he had a fundamental understanding of the latest manufacturing processes. During the 1860s and 1870s Dresser ran a large design studio, supplying numerous designs to many different manufacturers.

"As an ornamentist I have much the largest practice in the kingdom; so far as I know, there is not one branch of art-manufacture that I do not regularly design patterns for, and I hold regular appointments as 'art adviser' and 'chief designer' to several of our largest art-manufacturing firms" (1871). Because of Dresser's role as an art adviser, and the fact that he maintained such a large studio, it can sometimes be impossible to attribute a precise authorship to some objects. Dresser's job was often to supervise the overall quality of design in the products of a firm, and not necessarily to design them himself. At this stage of his career Dresser was working mostly for textile and wallpaper companies as an adviser and "ornamentist"; unfortunately, because of the perishable nature of textiles and wallpapers, most of this work has disappeared. The following quote from *Principles of Decorative Design* (1873) illustrates Dresser's approach to the use of materials: "If we propose to ourselves the formation of a sugar basin of semi-circular shape, of what thickness must the metal be in order that it may not bend when lifted? It is obvious that the vessel must not yield its shape to ordinary pressure, nor be subject to alterations of form when in ordinary use; but if it is to be formed throughout of metal of such thickness as will secure its retaining its shape, it will be costly and heavy, and an amount of metal will be used in its formation sufficient for the manufacture of two or three such articles. Instead of forming the vessel throughout of thick metal, we may construct it from a thin sheet of silver; but in order that it possess sufficient strength we must indent one or more beads on its side […] or we can form an angle by having a rim projecting into the basin […] or extending from it, thus give strength; but the two beads are more desirable, as the one gives strength at the top and the other at the lower portion of the vessel".

A page of designs from *The Technical Educator*, a popular magazine in which *Principles of Decorative Design* was first published as a series of articles.

PRINCIPLES OF DESIGN.—XXVI.
BY CHRISTOPHER DRESSER, PH.D., F.L.S., ETC.
SILVERSMITHS' WORK.

CONTINUING our consideration of hollow vessels, we have now to notice silversmiths' work, and here we may observe that while the material with which we have now to deal differs in character widely from that of which those vessels already considered have been formed, yet that many principles which have been enunciated are equally applicable to the objects now under consideration. Silver objects, like those formed of clay or glass, should perfectly serve the end for which they have been formed; also, the fact that ornament applied to rounded surfaces should be adapted for being viewed in perspective remains as binding on us as before; but herein the works of the silversmith differ from those already considered—they are formed of a material of intrinsic value, which is not the case with articles of earthenware or glass. Silver and gold being materials of considerable worth, it is necessary that the utmost economy be observed in using them, and in order to effect this a

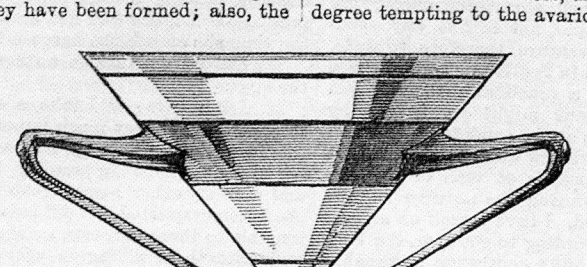

Fig. 122.

of costly substances, are of the utmost importance, and should be carefully thought out. If the designer forms works which are expensive, he places them beyond the reach of those who might otherwise enjoy them, and if heavy they appear clumsy in the hands of those accustomed to delicate and beautiful objects.

Besides this, works in silver and in gold are always in danger of being destroyed, owing to the intrinsic value of these metals; and if stolen, the theft is promptly hidden in the melting-pot. Now if we form the vessels of thin metal, we render the money value of the material less, and thus our works are to a smaller degree tempting to the avaricious, and their chance of longevity is greater. The precious metals are at all times perilous materials for the formation of works of art; but while we do use these worthy materials, let us so employ them as to give to our works every possible opportunity for long existence. If a work is to be so formed that it may exist for many years, it becomes of the highest importance that those objects which we create be well considered as to their utility, and at the same time beautiful in form. Long existence is an evil in the

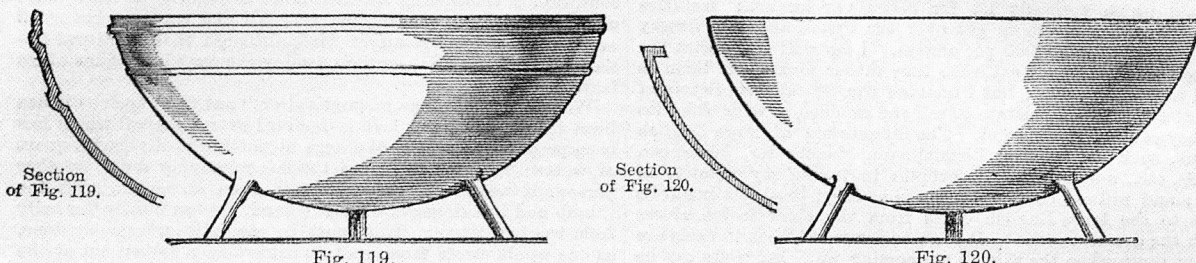

Section of Fig. 119.

Fig. 119.

Section of Fig. 120.

Fig. 120.

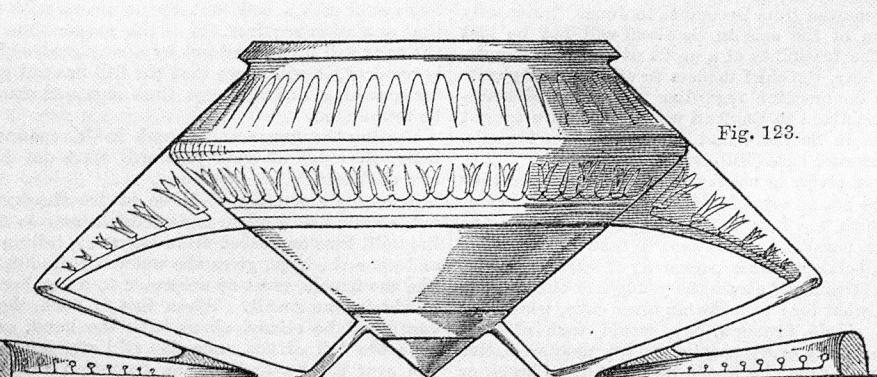

Fig. 123.

special mode of construction must be resorted to. If we propose to ourselves the formation of a sugar-basin of semi-circular shape, of what thickness must the metal be in order that it may not bend when lifted? It is obvious that the vessel must not yield its shape to ordinary pressure, nor be subject to alterations of form when in ordinary use; but if it is to be formed throughout of metal of such thickness as will secure its retaining its shape, it will be costly and heavy, and an amount of metal will be used in its formation sufficient for the manufacture of two or three such articles.

Instead of forming the vessel throughout of thick metal, we may construct it from a thin sheet of silver; but in order that it may possess sufficient strength we must indent one or more beads in its side (see Fig. 119); or we can form an angle by having a rim projecting into the basin (Fig. 120), or extending from it, and thus give strength; but the two beads are the more desirable, as the one gives strength at the top and the other at a lower portion of the vessel.

Modes of economising material, when we are forming vessels

case of an ugly object, or an ill-considered vessel; that which is not refining in its influence is better blotted out. Let that man who will not seek to embody beauty in his works make them heavy with metal, so that they may tempt the thief, and thus sooner blot out his works, as they tend only to debase and degrade; but he who loves refinement, and seeks to give chasteness of character to the objects which he creates, may well strive to secure to them length of duration.

There are various modes of working metal. It may be cast, hammered, cut, engraved, and manipulated in various ways.

Little that is satisfactory can result from casting. Casting is a rough means of producing a result, and at best achieves the formation of a mass which may be less troublesome to cut into shape than a more solid piece of metal; but casting without the application of other means of working metal achieves little of an art nature.

Some of the fine iron castings of Berlin are wonderfully good in their way, and are to an extent artistic; and certainly they contrast strangely with the cast handles and knobs which we often

1862–1880
Minton, Stoke on Trent

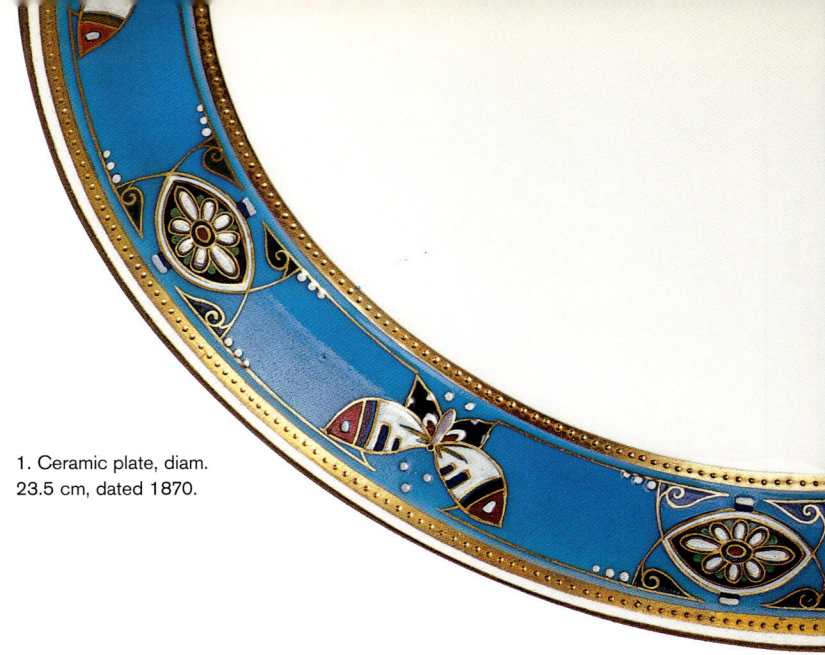

1. Ceramic plate, diam. 23.5 cm, dated 1870.

Founded in 1796 by Thomas Minton, Minton really built their reputation for excellence and innovation after 1836 when Thomas Minton's son, Herbert, took over. Herbert Minton pioneered the production of majolica, Parian ware, industrially produced encaustic tiles, and the introduction of pottery decorated using Collins and Reynolds patent lithographic process, examples of which were exhibited in Pugin's Medieval Court at the Great Exhibition. From the 1840s Minton adopted a policy of employing architect designers: this lead to the prestigious commission to supply designs by Pugin for the new Houses of Parliament as part of the architect's great scheme for the interior. After Herbert Minton's death in 1858, Minton was split into two parts: Minton Hollins & Co. for the tile production under the direction of Michael Daintry Hollins, and Minton & Co. for the chinaware and decorative tile production, under the direction of Robert Minton Campbell. Under the latter, Minton employed many designers including L. M. Solon, H. Stacy Marks, J. Moyr Smith, W. S. Coleman (also the director of the Minton Art Pottery at South Kensington 1869–74), and of course Christopher Dresser, who designed a number of the exhibits in the 1862 and 1867 Exhibitions, and was to act as both adviser and designer during the subsequent years.

Two designs for Minton. *Top*: a variation of the design on p. 59 for no. 17. *Bottom*: a design for a vase. The decoration was called by Dresser "Old Bogey" and illustrated by him in *Principles of Decorative Design*, 1873. See nos. 6 and 4.

Minton 1862–1880

2. Ceramic vase,
h. 12 cm, circa 1870.

3. Ceramic vase,
h. 12.2 cm, circa 1862.

4. Ceramic vase,
h. 26.5 cm, marked
no. 1342, circa 1867.

Minton 1862–1880

5. Ceramic vase,
h. 10 cm, circa 1867.

6. Ceramic vase,
h. 29 cm, circa 1870.

7. Ceramic vase, h. 50 cm, circa 1867.

8. Ceramic tile, 20.3 cm sq., registered 1870.

9. Ceramic tile, 20.3 cm sq., Minton registered 1870.

10. Ceramic tile, 18 cm sq., marked Minton Hollins, circa 1870.

11. Ceramic tile, 20.3 cm sq., circa 1870.

12. Ceramic tile, 20.3 cm sq., marked Minton, circa 1875.

13. Ceramic tile, 20.3 cm sq., marked Minton's China Works, circa 1875.

14. Ceramic tile, 20 cm sq., circa 1875.

15. Ceramic tile, 32.4 cm sq., dated 1867.

16. Pair of ceramic tiles, each 14.8 cm sq., dated 1866.

17. Ceramic bowl,
h. 21 cm, circa 1870.

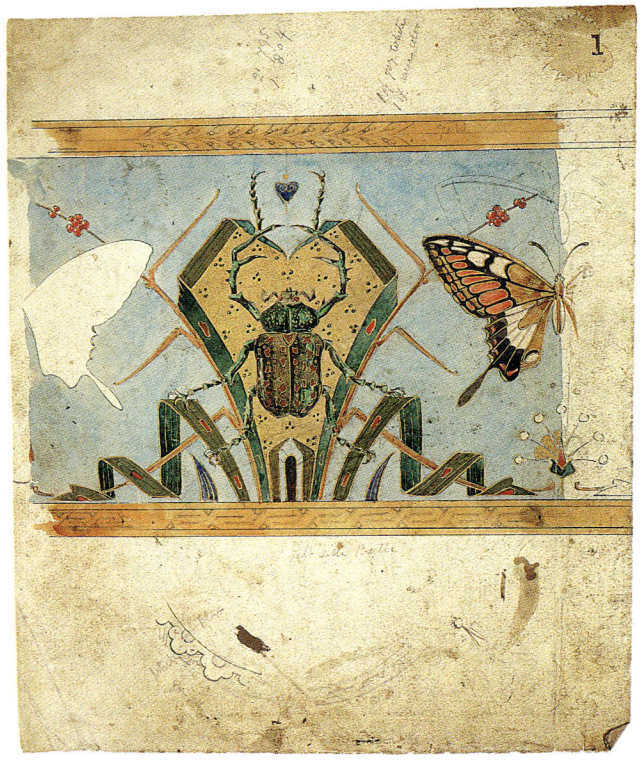

17. Ceramic bowl,
h. 21 cm, circa 1870.

Design for no. 17,
watercolour.

18. Two ceramic jugs
and a ceramic vase,
h. 15.2 cm each, circa
1873.

19. Ceramic vase, h. 14 cm, dated 1873.

20. Ceramic vase,
h. 22 cm, circa 1875.

21. *Left to right*: ceramic
spill vase, h. 18.5 cm,
marked Minton, circa
1872; ceramic spill vase,
h. 18.7 cm, dated 1873.

22. Ceramic vase,
circa 1867.

23. Ceramic vase,
h. 10.4 cm, circa 1870.

24. Ceramic vase,
h. 10.5 cm, circa 1870.

28. Ceramic cup, saucer
and plate, dated 1872.

Minton 1862–1880

25. Ceramic bowl, diam. 16.1 cm, circa 1870.

26. *Left to right*: ceramic cup and saucer, diam. 13.2 cm, marked Minton no. 2311, circa 1870; ceramic cup and saucer, diam. 13.7 cm, marked Minton no. 522, circa 1870.

27. Ceramic cup, saucer and plate, registered 1872.

29. Ceramic vase, h. 25 cm, circa 1870.

30. Ceramic vase, h. 25 cm, Minton's mark for 1873.

31. Ceramic vase, h. 25 cm, circa 1872.

Three designs by Dr Christopher Dresser for Minton, circa 1867.

66

Minton 1862–1880

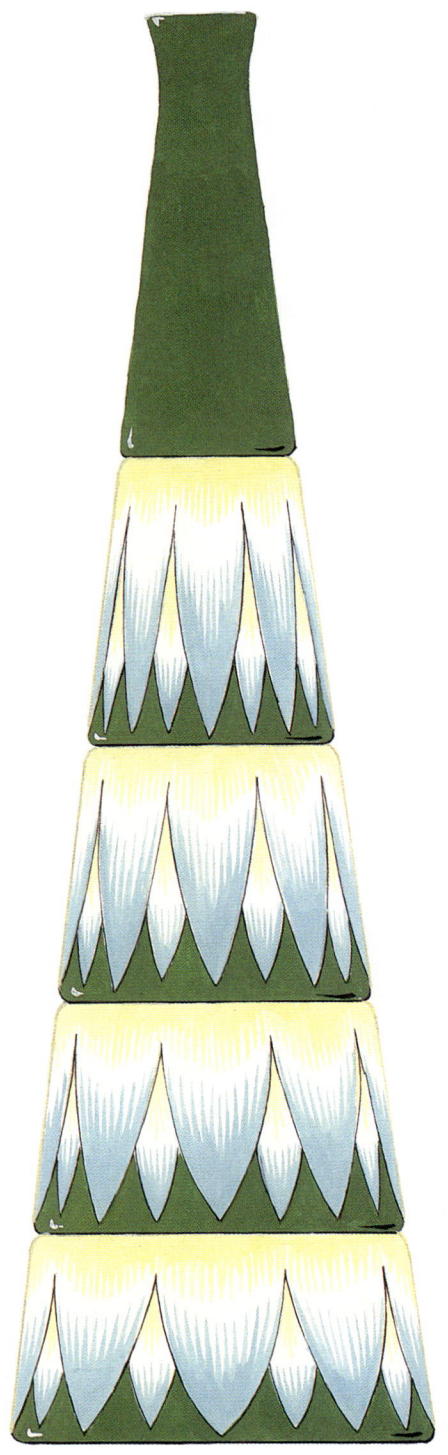

1866–1868
Josiah Wedgwood & Sons, Stoke on Trent

33. Ceramic vase, h. 25.5 cm, circa 1867.

32. Ceramic vase with enamel decoration, circa 1867.

Wedgwood was founded in 1759, and was one of the pioneering firms of the Industrial Revolution, exhibiting at all major International Exhibitions from 1851. The rising art movement and the arrival of the rediscovered arts of Japan shown at the London Exhibition of 1862 inspired the firm, under the direction of its art director Emile Lessore, to encourage experimentation in the new art pottery. The mid-1860s saw Godfrey Wedgwood employ a number of outside designers including Walter Crane and Christopher Dresser. Dresser was to introduce both new shapes and a whole new range of innovative decorative patterns to the factory. A surviving estimate book for 1866–68 shows an extensive range of Dresser designs available, which were applied widely to tableware, toilet ware, majolica and ground-laid wares. Many of these designs were continued until the close of the century. Dresser designs were exhibited on the Wedgwood stand in Paris in 1867 and in London in 1871.

34. Ceramic vase, circa 1867.

35. Terracotta flask,
h. 16.5 cm, marked
Wedgwood, circa 1867.

1869–1873
Watcombe Terracotta, Torquay

36. Terracotta plate with enamel decoration, circa 1872.

Watcombe was founded as an art pottery in South Devon in 1867 by G. J. Allen to exploit the unique local red clay, discovered by Allen when building Watcombe House. There is no documentary evidence that Dresser designed for Watcombe, but the circumstantial evidence is overwhelming; not only was terracotta one of Dresser's favourite materials at this stage of his career, but the shapes used by the firm were regularly used by Dresser throughout his career.

37. Blue glazed ceramic vase, h. 14.5 cm, circa 1880.

Opposite
38. Terracotta jug, h. 18 cm, marked Watcombe no. 457, circa 1872.

Watcombe Terracotta 1869–1873

39. Terracotta jug with silver mounts, h. 25 cm, marked Watcombe and registered 3 June 1872.

40. Terracotta vase, h. 34 cm, marked Watcombe Torquay 2223, circa 1875.

41. Terracotta teapot, h. 12 cm, marked Watcombe Torquay, circa 1875–80.

Watcombe Terracotta 1869–1873

42. Glazed terracotta vase, h. 13 cm, marked Watcombe no. 4040, circa 1872.

43. Glazed terracotta jug, h. 21.6 cm, marked Watcombe no. 5146, circa 1872.

44. Pair of glazed terracotta vases, h. 23 cm, marked Watcombe no. 4034, circa 1872.

1867–1872
Coalbrookdale, Shropshire

Founded in Shropshire in the early eighteenth century, Coalbrookdale was one of the most important pioneering companies of the Industrial Revolution, responsible for the casting of the first cast-iron bridge over Ironbridge Gorge in 1779. Coalbrookdale's fortunes declined in the early nineteenth century, until Abraham Darby IV and Alfred Darby took control in 1830. In 1834 they commenced the production of ornamental castings, employing John Bell (an associate of Henry Cole) as a designer. Bell's designs for Coalbrookdale were shown in the 1851 Exhibition and received much praise. They carried on this tradition and continued to employ designers throughout the century: Maurice B. Adams, B. J. Talbert, Alfred Stevens and of course Christopher Dresser. Dresser designed for Coalbrookdale from 1867, producing some of his most dramatic early work for them, and exhibiting in the 1871 London Exhibition. The medium of cast iron was well suited to Dresser's designs for ornament.

45. Cast iron and wood chair, marked Coalbrookdale, cipher for 8 March 1870.

Coalbrookdale 1867–1872

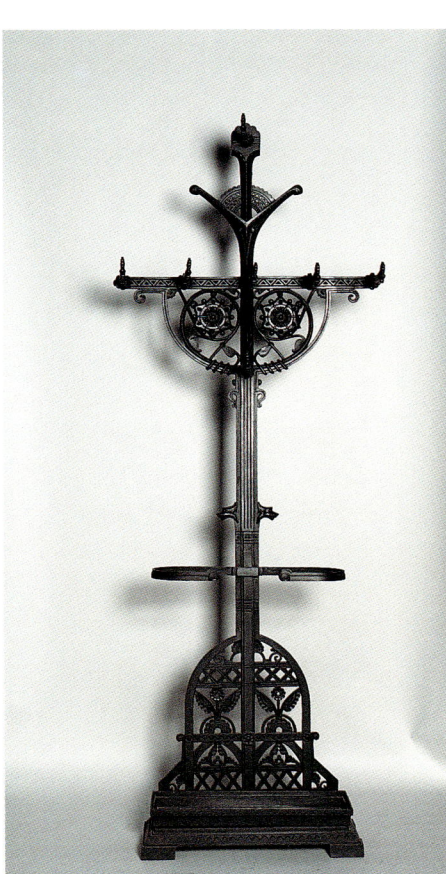

46. Cast iron hallstand, h. 190 cm, circa 1870.

47. Cast iron hallstand, h. 223 cm, circa 1870.

Right
48. Cast iron hallstand, circa 1867.

49. Cast iron hallstand, registered 8 March 1870.

50. Cast iron hall table, marked Coalbrookdale, cipher for 25 October 1869.

51. Cast iron garden bench, length 150 cm, circa 1870.

Opposite
52. Cast iron and wood chair of the Lily pattern, circa 1870.

Coalbrookdale 1867–1872

Dresser's Designs Subsequent to his Visit to Japan

In 1877 Christopher Dresser travelled to Japan, visiting the 1876 Centennial Exhibition in Philadelphia en route. Dresser was the first Western designer to visit the newly accessible Japan specifically to study its arts and industries (Japan had only allowed foreigners into their country since 1852). Dresser was treated as an official visitor, he was introduced to the emperor and given access to areas prohibited to foreigners. He visited 68 pottery manufacturers, and scores of manufacturers in other industries, seeing and understanding how everyday things made out of seemingly humble materials could be beautiful. Dresser writes in his book *Japan*: "There is as much pride in Japan manifested by the maker in completing a little cup, a lacquer box, a sheet of leather paper, or even a pair of chopsticks and by perfect work any handicraftsman may attain to the celebrity enjoyed here by a Landseer, a Turner, or an Owen Jones, and the fame supplies a stimulus for the production of work still more excellent."
He had 1,000 photographs taken and visited 100 temples; altogether Dresser stayed in Japan for four months.

It is instructive to note that, in the sale of his possessions on his death, among his belongings there was almost nothing of European origin: thus his inspiration was an eclectic mix of the world's cultures. Dresser's collection was described as follows: "A Catalogue of the most interesting and miscellaneous Collection of Curios formed by the late Dr Dresser, consisting of metal work, lacquer, bamboo, enamels, carved stone from China and Japan, Persian & Indian glass, earthenware and tiles, Pottery from the south of France, Jamaica, Siberia and other parts; Roumanian woodwork, and a great variety of curios from Africa, New Zealand, Egypt and other countries".

On his return to England Dresser's work changed dramatically. He embarked on a series of extraordinary designs for the silver makers Hukin and Heath, shortly followed by an even more daring series for James Dixon & Sons and a radical group of pottery designs for Linthorpe. In 1880 Dresser set up his most ambitious venture yet, the Art Furnishers' Alliance; this sought to provide everything necessary for the artistic house. Unfortunately the Alliance was not successful financially and closed in 1883. At about the same time Dresser also ceased working for Hukin and Heath, James Dixon & Sons and Linthorpe. He moved from central London to suburban Sutton, and although he was still to design some important things, notably silver for Elkington and Clutha glass for James Couper, his most remarkable work was behind him.

Four pages from James Dixon & Sons 1879 cost book showing Dresser's designs.

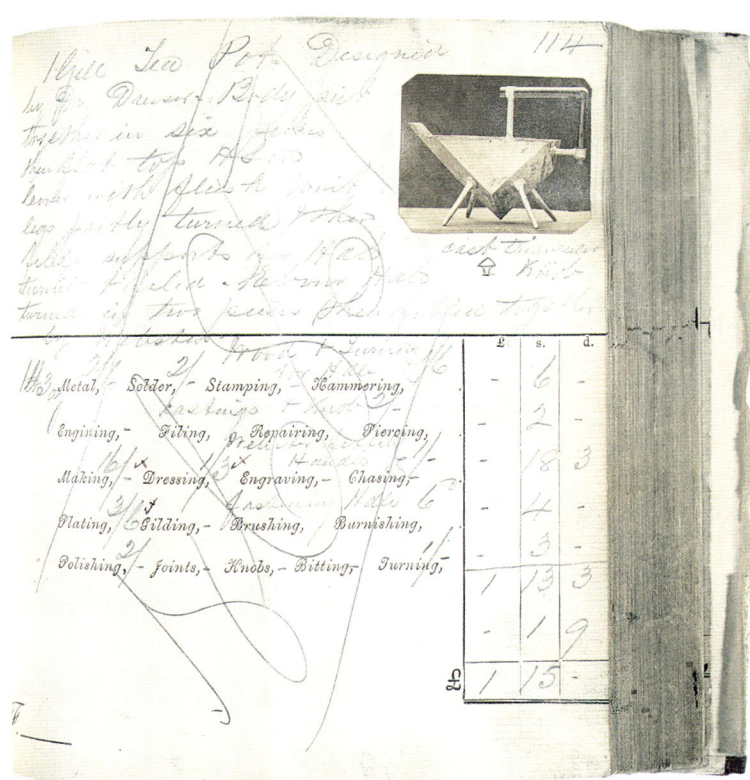

1878–1883
Hukin and Heath, Birmingham and London

53. Silver-plated letter rack, h. 14.5 cm, marked H&H 2589, registered 1881.

Founded in Birmingham in 1855, Hukin and Heath specialized in novelty ware, supplying retail outlets such as Asprey and Co., Walter Thornhill, and Alfred Clark of Bond Street. Hukin and Heath seem to have been the first company to employ Dresser on his return from Japan in 1877 or 1878, and held a sensational exhibition of his radical new designs in August 1879 at their new premises, 19 Charterhouse Street. This also appears to be the first time that Dresser's name was prominently marked on objects that he had designed. He was associated with the company until at least 1881; they were creditors of the Art Furnishers' Alliance in 1883. Hukin and Heath were periodically to produce designs in the style of Dresser, with one notable group realized at the beginning of the 1890s. It is not known whether Dresser had any connection with these later products.

Hukin and Heath 1878–1883

54. Silver-plated metal and glass decanter set, h. 33 cm, marked H&H 1936, circa 1880.

55. Silver-plate and ebony three-piece tea set, teapot h. 11 cm, stamped "Designed by Dr C Dresser", registration mark for 1878.

56. Silver, bone and enamel teapot, h. 10 cm, stamped "Designed by Dr C Dresser", Birmingham silver marks for 1878, registration mark for 1878.

57. Silver-plated toast rack, h. 14 cm, stamped "Designed by Dr C Dresser", registered 1878.

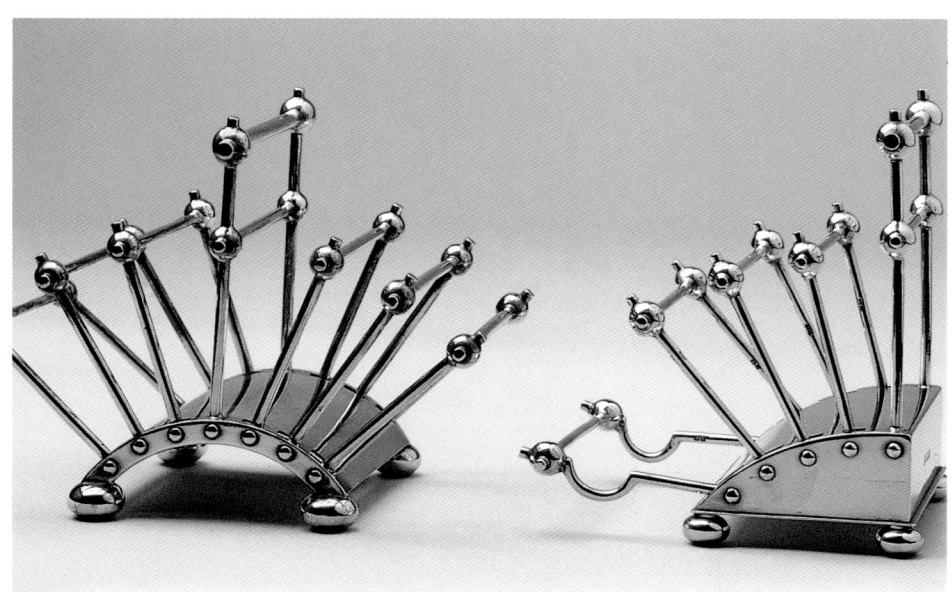

58. *Left to right*: silver-plated letter rack, h. 12 cm, marked H&H 2555, registered 1881; silver letter rack, circa 1881.

Opposite
59. Silver-plated toast rack, h. 14 cm, stamped "Designed by Dr C Dresser", marked H&H 1987, registered 1878.

Hukin and Heath 1878–1883

60. Silver-plate and glass holder, h. 17 cm, stamped "Designed by Dr C Dresser", marked H&H, registered 1879.

Hukin and Heath 1878–1883

61. Silver-plate and glass cruet set, h. 13.5 cm, marked H&H 2239, registered 1879.

62. Silver-plated milk and sugar set, h. 16 cm, marked H&H, register number 18367 for 1885.

63. Silver-plate, glass and ebony Tantalus, h. 29 cm, stamped "Designed by Dr C Dresser", marked H&H 2046, registered 1879.

64. Silver-plate and glass cruet set, h. 23 cm, stamped "Designed by Dr C Dresser", marked H&H 1873, registered 1879.

65. Silver-plate and ebony spoonwarmer, h. 12.5 cm, marked H&H 2887, circa 1880.

66. Silver-plated warmer, h. 7.3 cm, stamped "Designed by Dr C Dresser", marked H&H, registered 1878.

67. Silver-plate and ebony kettle on stand, h. 18 cm, marked H&H, registered 1878.

68. Silver-plated picnic set, marked H&H, registered 1879.

Hukin and Heath 1878–1883

69. Silver-plated bowl and cover, h. 20 cm, stamped "Designed by Dr C Dresser", circa 1880.

90

Hukin and Heath 1878–1883

71. Silver and glass cruet set, h. 9.3 cm, hallmarks for 1884–85.

72. Silver-plate and glass cruet set, h. 15 cm, stamped "Designed by Dr C Dresser", marked H&H 1867, registration mark for 1878.

73. Silver-plate and glass cruet set, h. 21 cm, stamped "Designed by Dr C Dresser", marked H&H 1918, registered 1878.

70. Silver-plate and glass cruet set, h. 21 cm, stamped "Designed by Dr C Dresser", marked H&H 1953, 1878.

74. Silver-plate and glass cruet set, h. 18.7 cm, stamped "Designed by Dr C Dresser", marked H&H, registered 1878.

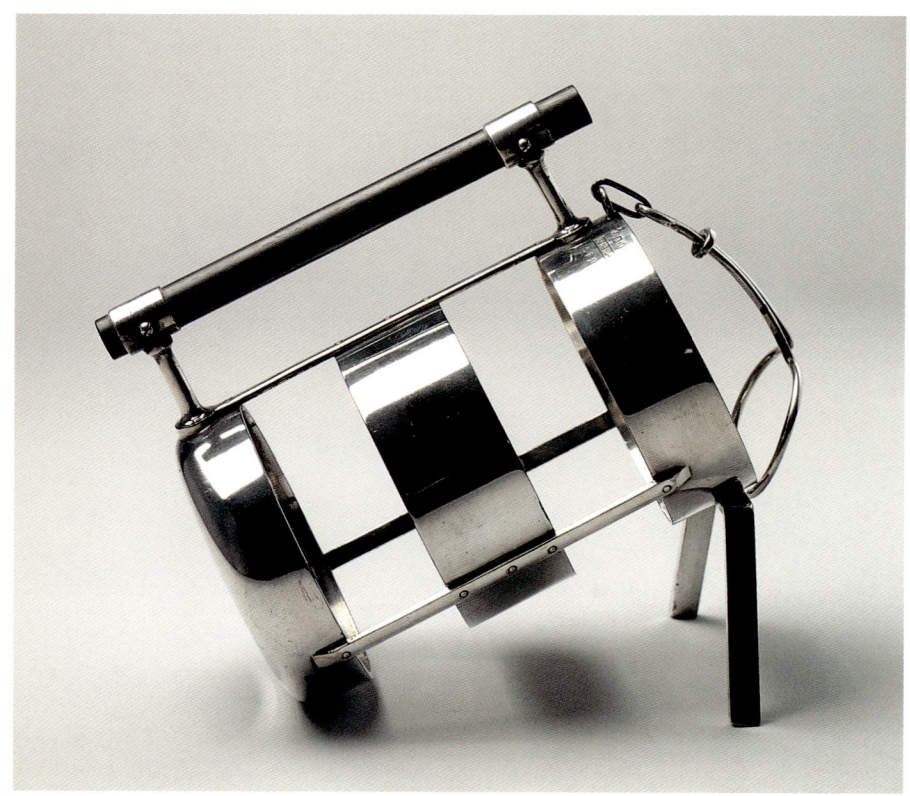

75. Silver-plate and ebony wine bottle holder, h. 18 cm, marked H&H 3128, register number 1343 for 1885.

76. Silver-plate and glass decanter, h. 18 cm, marked H&H 2120, circa 1880.

Opposite
77. Silver-plate and ebony spoonwarmer, h. 15 cm, marked H&H 2857, circa 1880.

78. Silver-plate and glass decanter, h. 23 cm, stamped "Designed by Dr C Dresser", marked H&H 2045, registration mark for 1879.

79. Silver-plate and ebony soup tureen and ladle, h. 21 cm, stamped "Designed by Dr C Dresser", marked H&H 2123, registration mark for 1880.

80. Silver sugar bowl and spoon, h. 14.2 cm, marked Heath and Middleton, hallmarks for 1883.

81. Silver-plate and wood tureen, h. 21.8 cm, stamped "Designed by Dr C Dresser", marked H&H, registered 1881.

82. Silver-plate and wood wine bottle holder, h. 20 cm, marked H&H, registered 1881.

83. Silver-plate, glass and ebony decanter, circa 1880.

85. Silver-plate, glass and ebony decanter, h. 22.5 cm, registered 1881.

86. *Left to right*: silver and glass decanter, h. 24.5 cm, marked Heath and Middleton, London, hallmark for 1882–83; silver-plate, glass and ebony decanter, h. 22 cm, circa 1881; silver, glass and ebony decanter, h. 22.5 cm, marked Heath and Middleton, London, hallmark for 1882–83.

84. Silver-plated bowl,
width 14 cm, signed,
marked H&H 2072.

1879–1882
James Dixon & Sons, Sheffield

Founded about 1806 in Sheffield, James Dixon & Sons took out a licence from Elkington in 1848 for the new electroplating process. Dresser started to work for Dixon from 1879 and produced perhaps the most daring of all his designs for them; all works were invariably marked with a facsimile signature. Dixon were also shareholders in the Art Furnishers' Alliance. As with Hukin and Heath, Dixon carried on producing designs in the Dresser style without his obvious endorsement, and certainly one design in the 1882 cost book that does not bear his name, was later sold by him to Elkington.

James Dixon & Sons, a photograph of a decanter from a contemporary record book.

87. Silver-plate and glass decanter, h. 31.3 cm, signed, marked James Dixon & Sons, circa 1879.

James Dixon & Sons 1879–1882

James Dixon & Sons, photographs from a contemporary record book showing a variety of teapots.

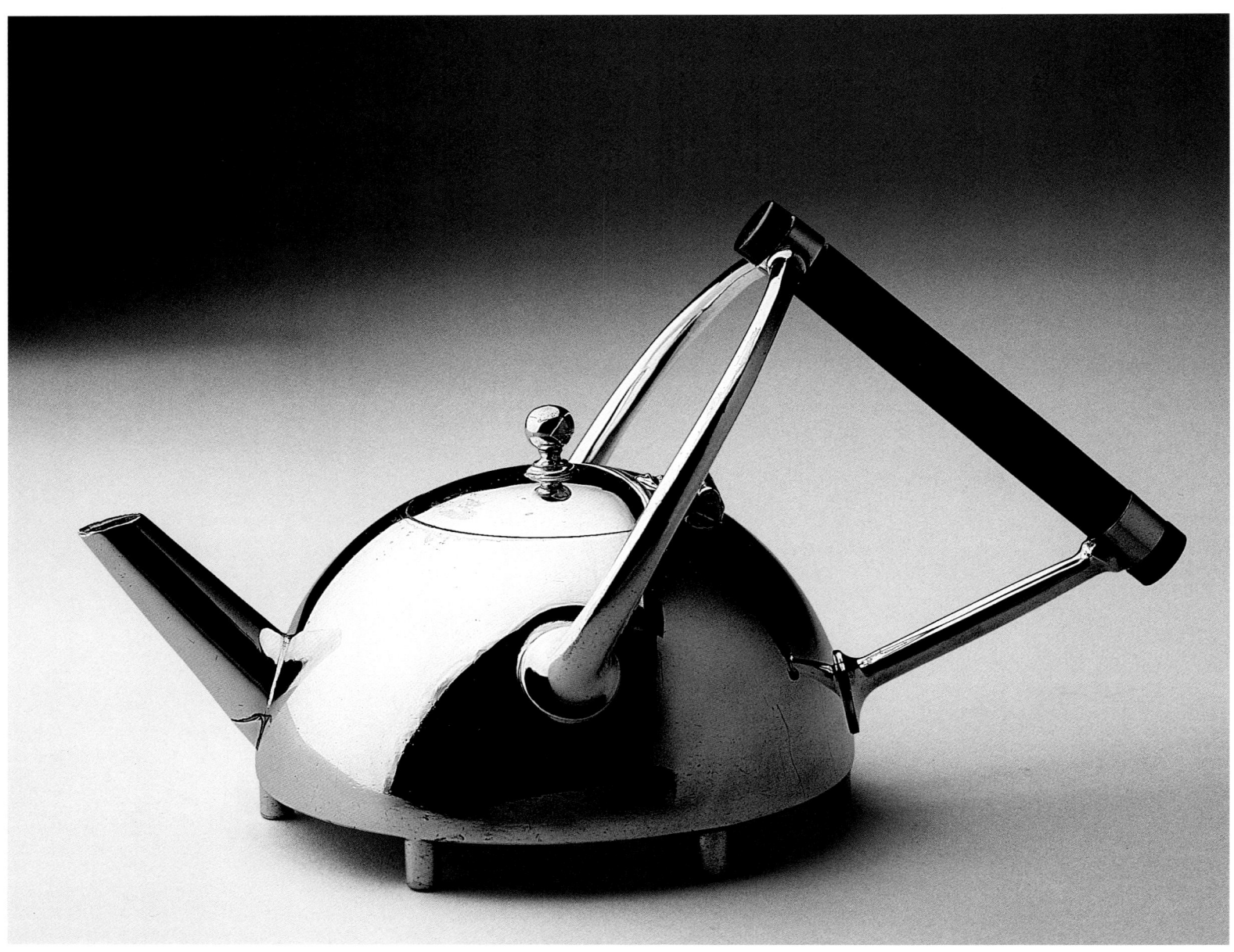

88. Silver-plate and ebony teapot, h. 13.4 cm, signed, registered 1879.

89. Silver-plate and ebony teapot, h. 17 cm, signed, marked James Dixon & Sons 2274, circa 1879.

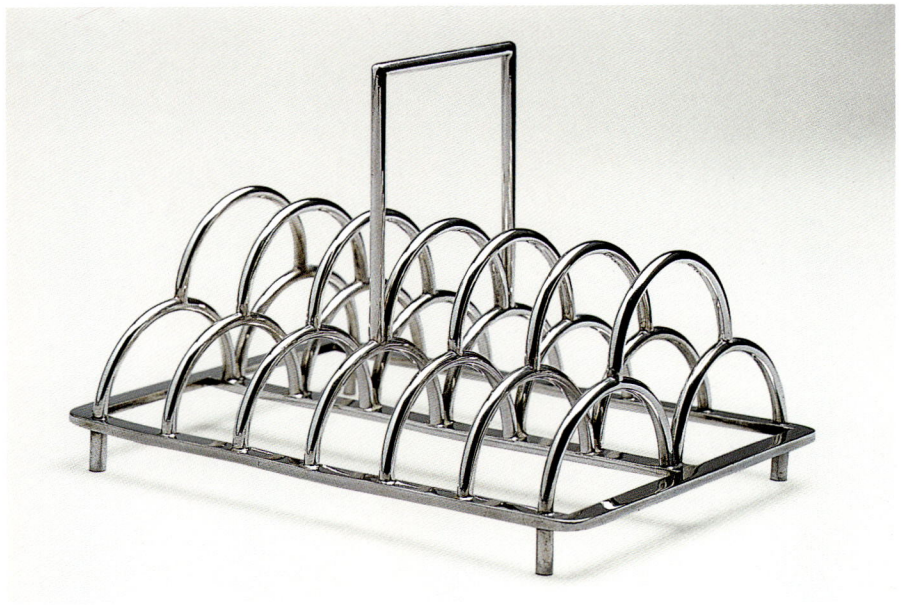

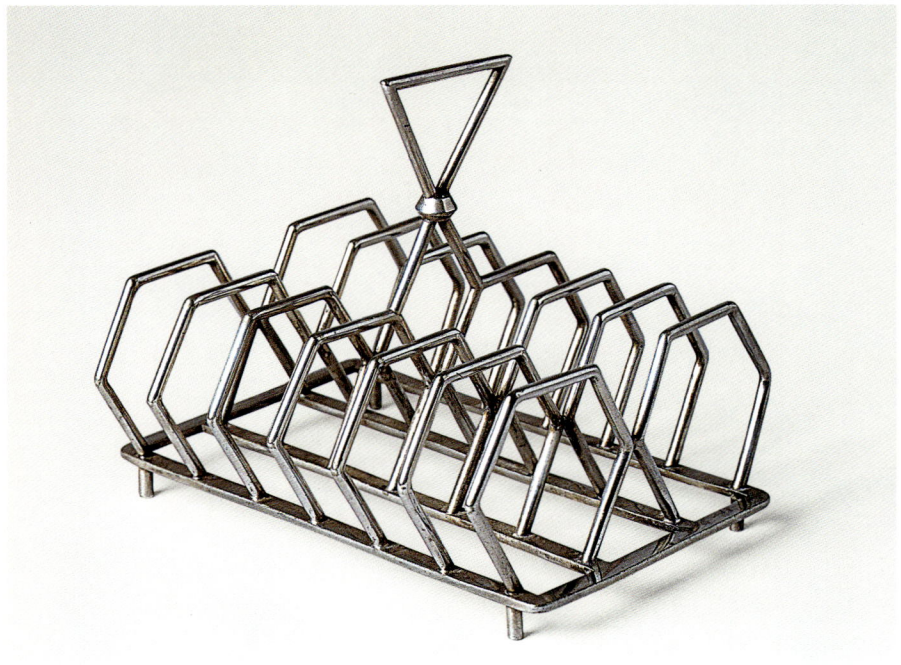

90. Silver-plated toast rack, h. 11.5 cm, signed, circa 1880.

92. Silver-plated toast rack, h. 13.3 cm, signed, marked James Dixon & Sons no. 68, circa 1879.

91. Silver-plated toast rack, h. 15.3 cm, marked no. 72, circa 1879.

93. Silver-plated egg and toast holder, h. 16 cm, signed, marked no. 115, circa 1879.

94. Silver-plated toast rack, h. 14 cm, illegible marks, 1879.

95. Silver-plate and ebony three-piece tea set, h. 14 cm, signed, marked James Dixon & Sons 2278, registered 1880.

96. Silver-plate and ebony toast rack, length 27 cm, signed, marked James Dixon & Sons 963, circa 1879.

97. Silver-plate and glass decanter, h. 24.5 cm, signed, marked James Dixon & Sons 2548, circa 1879.

James Dixon & Sons 1879–1882

98. Glass and silver-plated decanter, h. 26 cm, signed, marked James Dixon & Sons, circa 1880.

99. Silver-plated tea set, signed, registered 1880.

100. Silver-plate and ebony teapot, h. 11 cm, signed, marked James Dixon & Sons, registered 1880.

1879–1882
Linthorpe Pottery, Middlesbrough

101. Ceramic pitcher, h. 24.5 cm, signed, marked no. 346 HT, circa 1880.

First producing pottery in 1879, Linthorpe was set up at Middlesbrough in Teesside as an art manufacturers complex, however art pottery only seems to have been made. In choosing Teesside, Dresser was reputedly moved by the plight of the local unemployed, and, after his experiences in Japan, the humble local brick clay would have seemed an ideal material with which to make art pottery. An entrepreneur, John Harrison, funded Linthorpe and was later to become a director of the Art Furnishers' Alliance. Chosen by Dresser as manager, Henry Tooth had no previous experience in running a pottery, and was apprenticed to the Derbyshire potters T. G. Green for a few months in 1878 to learn the necessary skills. Linthorpe pottery was unlike anything seen before, exploiting the plasticity of clay and combining it with abstract glazes. The shapes were not only inspired by Japan, but also by civilizations as far apart as Morocco and Peru. Dresser's designs were all marked with a facsimile signature. Dresser and Holme, importers of Japanese ware, were the sole agents for Linthorpe, and Dresser promoted their wares in his magazine *Furniture Gazette*. Dresser ceased his association with Linthorpe in 1882, as subsequently did Henry Tooth. After Dresser's departure, Linthorpe continued to produce shapes by him and even introduced some new ones previously designed by him but not put into production. When Linthorpe closed on Harrison's death in 1889, the moulds were auctioned and bought by other potteries, including Ault and the Torquay Terracotta Company.

102. Two ceramic vases, h. 30.5 cm, signed, marked no. 157, the one on the right monogrammed HT, circa 1880.

103. Ceramic vase, h. 43 cm, signed, Linthorpe mark, circa 1880.

Linthorpe Pottery 1879–1882

104. *Left to right*: ceramic "Peruvian" vessel, h. 10 cm, signed, marked no. 344 HT, circa 1880; ceramic "Peruvian" vessel, h. 10 cm, signed, marked no. 315 HT, circa 1880.

105. Two ceramic flasks, h. 13 cm, marked no. 440, circa 1880.

106. Ceramic vase, h. 49.5 cm, signed, marked no. 827 HT, circa 1880.

Linthorpe Pottery 1879–1882

Opposite
107. Ceramic vase,
h. 23.5 cm, signed, marked
no. 536 HT, circa 1880.

108. *Left to right*: ceramic
pitcher, h. 28 cm, signed,
marked no. 576 HT,
circa 1880; ceramic
coffeepot, h. 27 cm,
signed, marked no. 664 HT,
circa 1880.

109. Ceramic vase,
h. 31.2 cm, signed,
no. 452 HT, circa 1880.

110. Ceramic vase,
h. 35.5 cm, signed,
monogrammed twice HT,
circa 1880.

111. Ceramic "Peruvian" pitcher, h. 17 cm, signed, marked no. 296 HT, circa 1880.

112. Ceramic spill vase, h. 14 cm, signed, marked no. 175 HT, circa 1880.

113. Ceramic vase, h. 26.5 cm, signed, marked HT, circa 1880.

114. Ceramic vase, h. 23.5 cm, signed, marked no. 538 HT, circa 1880.

115. Ceramic vase, h. 20.5 cm, signed, marked no. 223 HT, circa 1880.

Linthorpe Pottery 1879–1882

Linthorpe Pottery 1879–1882

117. *Left to right*: ceramic vase, h. 13.7 cm, signed, marked no. 138 HT, circa 1880; ceramic vase, h. 24.2 cm, signed, marked no. 44 HT, circa 1880; ceramic vase, h. 18 cm, signed, marked no. 141 HT, circa 1880.

118. Ceramic vase/sake bottle, circa 1880.

119. Ceramic vase, h. 23 cm, signed, marked no. 24 HT, circa 1880.

116. Ceramic vase, h. 41.5 cm, signed, marked HT, circa 1880.

120. Ceramic vase, h. 31 cm, signed, circa 1880.

121. Ceramic jar and cover, h. 17 cm, signed, marked no. 277 HT, circa 1880.

122. Ceramic vase, h. 19 cm, signed, marked no. 331, circa 1880.

123. *Left to right*: ceramic vase, h. 16.5 cm, signed, marked no. 18, circa 1880; ceramic dish, width 19.5 cm, signed, marked no. 276, circa 1880.

125. Ceramic unglazed pitcher, h. 24 cm, signed, marked Linthorpe 686, circa 1880.

124. *Left to right*: ceramic vase, h. 18.3 cm, signed, marked no. 848, circa 1880; ceramic vase, h. 21 cm, signed, marked no. 83 HT, circa 1880; ceramic vase, h. 24.2 cm, signed, marked no. 346, circa 1880.

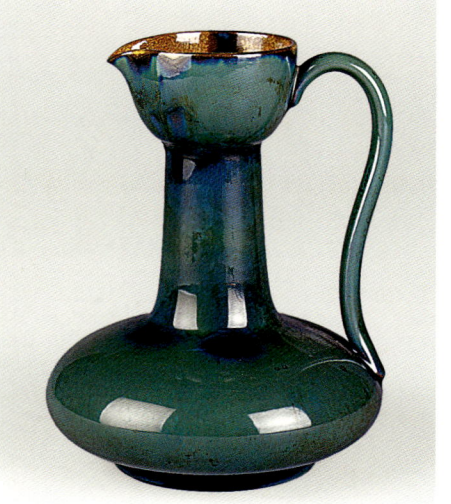

126. *Left to right*: Linthorpe ceramic pitcher, h. 19 cm, signed, marked no. 311 HT, circa 1880; Ault ceramic pitcher, h. 18 cm, marked no. 138, circa 1890.

127. Ceramic pitcher, h. 18 cm, signed, marked no. 18 HT, circa 1880.

128. Ceramic pitcher, signed, circa 1880.

Opposite
129. Ceramic jug, signed, circa 1880.

Linthorpe Pottery 1879–1882

130. Ceramic pitcher,
h. 17.7 cm, signed, marked
no. 610 HT, circa 1880.

131. Ceramic "Peruvian"
pitcher, h. 12 cm, signed,
marked no. 335 HT,
circa 1880.

132. Ceramic pitcher,
h. 18.5 cm, signed,
marked no. 551 HT,
circa 1880.

Linthorpe Pottery 1879–1882

133. Ceramic vase, h. 21 cm, signed, monogrammed HT, circa 1880.

134. *Left to right*: ceramic spill vase, h. 15.5 cm, signed, marked no. 175 HT, circa 1880; ceramic vase, h. 17.8 cm, signed, marked no. 244 HT, circa 1880.

135. Ceramic pitcher, h. 21.5 cm, signed, marked no. 611 HT, circa 1880.

Linthorpe Pottery 1879–1882

Linthorpe Pottery 1879–1882

136. Ceramic vase, h. 45 cm, signed, Linthorpe mark, circa 1880.

137. *Left to right*: ceramic pitcher, h. 18.5 cm, signed, marked no. 347 HT, circa 1880; ceramic "Peruvian" pitcher, h. 17 cm, signed, no. 296 HT, circa 1880; ceramic "Peruvian" pitcher, h. 19.5 cm, signed, marked no. 613 HT, circa 1880.

138. Ceramic vase, h. 10 cm, signed, marked Linthorpe 281, circa 1880.

139. Ceramic pitcher, circa 1883.

140. Ceramic jug with stopper, signed, circa 1880.

141. Ceramic vase, h. 10.5 cm, signed, marked no. 330 HT, circa 1880.

142. Ceramic vase, h. 10.5 cm, signed, circa 1880.

143. Ceramic plate,
diam. 34 cm, signed,
circa 1880.

144. Ceramic jar
and cover, h. 23.5 cm,
signed, circa 1880.

145. Ceramic plate,
diam. 26.4 cm, signed,
circa 1881.

146. Ceramic plate,
diam. 29.2 cm, signed,
circa 1881.

147. Ceramic vase, h. 37 cm, signed, circa 1880.

Linthorpe Pottery 1879–1882

148. Ceramic vase,
h. 47 cm, signed,
circa 1880.

149. Ceramic bowl,
h. 13 cm, signed,
circa 1880.

150. *Left to right*:
terracotta vase, h. 16 cm,
signed, marked Linthorpe,
circa 1880; terracotta
vase, h. 22 cm, signed,
marked Linthorpe 270,
circa 1880.

151. Ceramic vase,
h. 20 cm, signed, marked
Linthorpe 223,
circa 1880.

152. Ceramic vase,
h. 20 cm, circa 1880.

153. *Left to right*: ceramic vase, h. 20 cm, signed, marked no. 393 HT, circa 1880; ceramic vase, h. 27.2 cm, signed, marked no. 692 HT, circa 1880.

154. Ceramic vase,
h. 25.5 cm, signed,
marked no. 301 HT,
circa 1880.

155. Ceramic vase,
h. 48 cm, signed, marked
no. 827 HT, circa 1880.

156. Ceramic dish, diam.
13.4 cm, signed, marked
no. 286 HT, circa 1880.

158. Ceramic dish, length
29 cm, signed, circa
1880.

157. Ceramic vase,
h. 22.5 cm, signed,
circa 1890.

159. Ceramic vase, h. 23 cm, signed, circa 1880.

160. Ceramic vase, h. 23.5 cm, signed, monogrammed HT, circa 1880.

161. Pair of ceramic vases, h. 47 cm, signed, marked no. 168 HT, circa 1880.

162. Ceramic sake bottle, h. 13.4 cm, signed, marked no. 341, circa 1880.

163. Ceramic vase, h. 22.5 cm, signed, marked no. 424, circa 1880.

164. Ceramic vase, h. 30.5 cm, signed, marked no. 157, circa 1880.

165. Ceramic vase, h. 19.5 cm, signed, marked no. 298 HT, circa 1880.

166. Ceramic "Peruvian" vase, h. 20 cm, signed, marked no. 393 HT, circa 1880.

167. Ceramic vase, h. 19.6 cm, signed, marked no. 326 HT, circa 1880.

1872–1893
Benham and Froud, London

168. Copper and brass kettle, h. 21 cm, marked Benham and Froud, circa 1882.

Manufacturers of copper and brass in Chandos Street, London, Benham and Froud exhibited at Paris (1855) and London (1862) Exhibitions. Dresser designed sporadically for the firm from about 1872 to 1893, and they supplied the Art Furnishers' Alliance with wooden coalboxes and brass and copper ware, some of which are documented in photographs in the Chubb Archives.

This photograph from the Chubb Archive shows metalwork at the Art Furnishers' Alliance, circa 1880–83. Benham and Froud was probably the manufacturer of most of the objects.

Opposite
169. Copper and brass ewer, h. 31 cm, marked Benham and Froud, circa 1885.

170. Copper and brass kettle, h. 19 cm, circa 1885.

171. Brass bottle, h. 22.5 cm, marked Benham and Froud, circa 1885.

172. Copper kettle with wooden handle, h. 26 cm, marked Benham and Froud, circa 1885.

173. Copper and brass coffeepot, circa 1882.

174. Copper and brass kettle, h. 20 cm, circa 1880.

Benham and Froud 1872–1893

175. Copper tray overlaid with other metals, diam. 32 cm, marked Benham and Froud, circa 1885.

176. Copper and brass ewer, h. 13 cm, marked Benham and Froud, circa 1875–85.

177. Brass ewer, h. 16 cm, marked Benham and Froud, circa 1885.

178. Copper and brass candlestick, h. 27.5 cm, sold by the Art Furnishers' Alliance and made by Benham and Froud, circa 1880.

179. Jardinière made of mixed metals, circa 1880.

180. Copper pitcher, h. 23 cm, signed on the base in indelible ink, 1875–85. This appears to be a prototype. The maker is unknown.

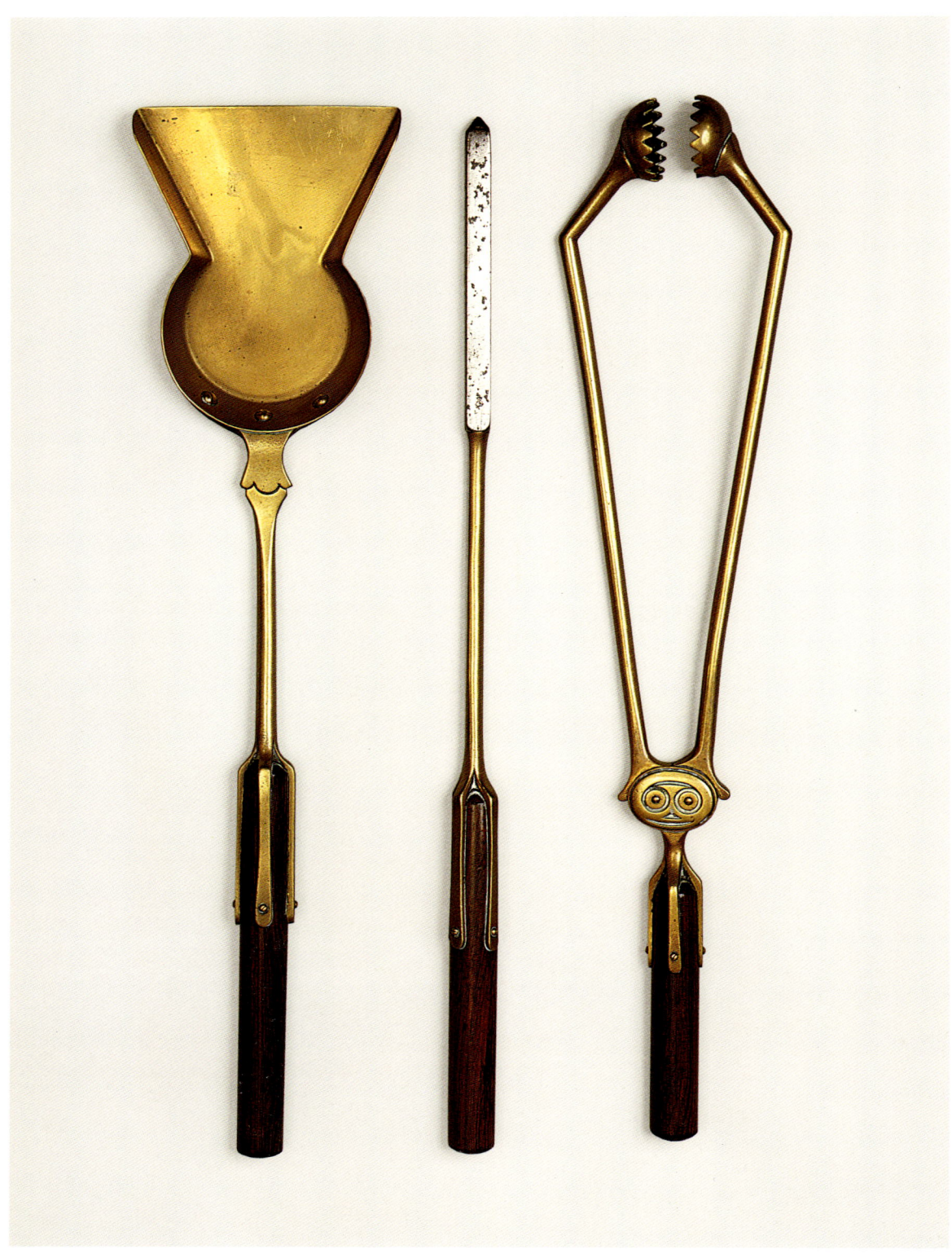

181. Set of three wood and brass fire irons, length 62 cm, mark for Benham and Froud, circa 1880.

182. Large mixed metal jardinière, h. 47 cm, circa 1882.

1880–1883

Art Furnishers' Alliance Co., New Bond Street, London

183. Painted wood fan, circa 1880. The decoration is a variant of a plate in *Studies in Design*.

The Art Furnishers' Alliance was an association of art manufacturers founded by Christopher Dresser in 1880 to supply "whatever is necessary to the complete artistic furnishing of a house". Dresser was employed as art director and the directors were George Hayter Chubb, John Harrison, Edward Cope and Sir Edward Lee. The furniture was made on Chubb's premises and the stock included: Oriental objects by Arthur Liberty, Dresser and Holme; silverware by Hukin and Heath and James Dixon & Sons; wallpaper by Lightbown and Aspinal, Jeffrey, Scott Cuthbertson and Arthur Sanderson; linoleum and wallpapers by Frederick Walton; glass by Sowerby; metalwork by Benham and Froud; carpets by John Brinton; pottery by Linthorpe. A number of the suppliers were also shareholders, including Harrison (Linthorpe), Chubb, Dixon and Liberty. The Art Furnishers' Alliance went into liquidation in 1883, and their stock was auctioned off. The demise of the Art Furnishers' Alliance marked the end of Dresser's ambition to create a store in London's most prestigious street, which could provide everything for the artistic house.

Photographs from the Chubb Archive showing furniture from the Art Furnishers' Alliance, circa 1880–83.

Art Furnishers' Alliance Co. 1880–1883

184. Chair made of wood with gilded decoration for the Art Furnishers' Alliance, circa 1880.

185. Upholstered armchair made for the Art Furnishers' Alliance.

186. Wooden coalbox made by Benham and Froud, h. 41 cm, 1875–80.

187. Ebonized dining chair, a variant on a model used in Bushloe House, circa 1875.

188. Slate fireplace with gilded decoration, circa 1875. The design of this fireplace is very close to those in Bushloe House and Allangate.

Art Furnishers' Alliance Co. 1880–1883

189. Ebonized wood coalbox, h. 41 cm, circa 1880.

190. Armchair made of straight sections of wood in a triangulated construction, made for the Art Furnishers' Alliance, circa 1880.

191. Ebonized wood chair possibly made by W. Booty of London, circa 1875.

192. Ebonized and gilded wood chair, circa 1880.

193. Ebonized wood chair made for the Art Furnishers' Alliance, circa 1880.

1865–1890
Elkington & Co., Birmingham and London

Elkington & Co. was founded between 1829 and 1836 by two cousins: George Richard Elkington and Henry Elkington. The Elkingtons took out three patents in 1836 and 1837 relating to electroplating, and in order to commercially exploit these, they formed a subsidiary partnership in 1837 with the button makers Hardman & Illiffe, who incidentally were chosen in the same year by A. W. N. Pugin to be his metalworkers. Electroplate was to take over very quickly from the previously dominant form of substitute silver, Sheffield plate, where a thin sheet of silver was fused to a base metal. Another relative of electroplating was electrotyping, where the mould itself was plated until a solid was formed; this process lent itself to the making of historic reproductions. Elkington's main designers were French: Emile Jeannest, Leonard Morel-Ladeuil and Albert Willms, the head of the design studio from 1859–99. Christopher Dresser was connected with Elkington from about 1865–90 and, apart from the famous series of designs from the 1880s, also seems to have been involved at least in an advisory capacity with their experiments with Japanese techniques such as Cloisonné and Komai ware.

194. Silver-plated tea set, marked Elkington & Co., registered 22863, 1885.

195. Silver-plated soup tureen with ebonized handles, h. 16.7 cm, marked Elkington & Co., 1885.

A page of designs from an Elkington's pattern book, 1885. Birmingham Library.

196. Silver-plated three-piece tea set. Teapot h. 11 cm, marked Elkington, registered 1885.

197. Silver-plate and glass cruet set, h. 14.8 cm, marked Elkington, registered 1885.

198. Silver-plated coffeepot, h. 23.8 cm, registered mark for 1885.

Elkington & Co. 1865–1890

Opposite
199. Silver-plated jug, h. 24 cm, marked Elkington 17558, register no. 22872, dated 1885.

200. Silver milk jug, h. 6.5 cm, marked Elkington & Co., registered 22865 for 1885.

Detail from a page of designs in an Elkington's silver pattern book, 1885.

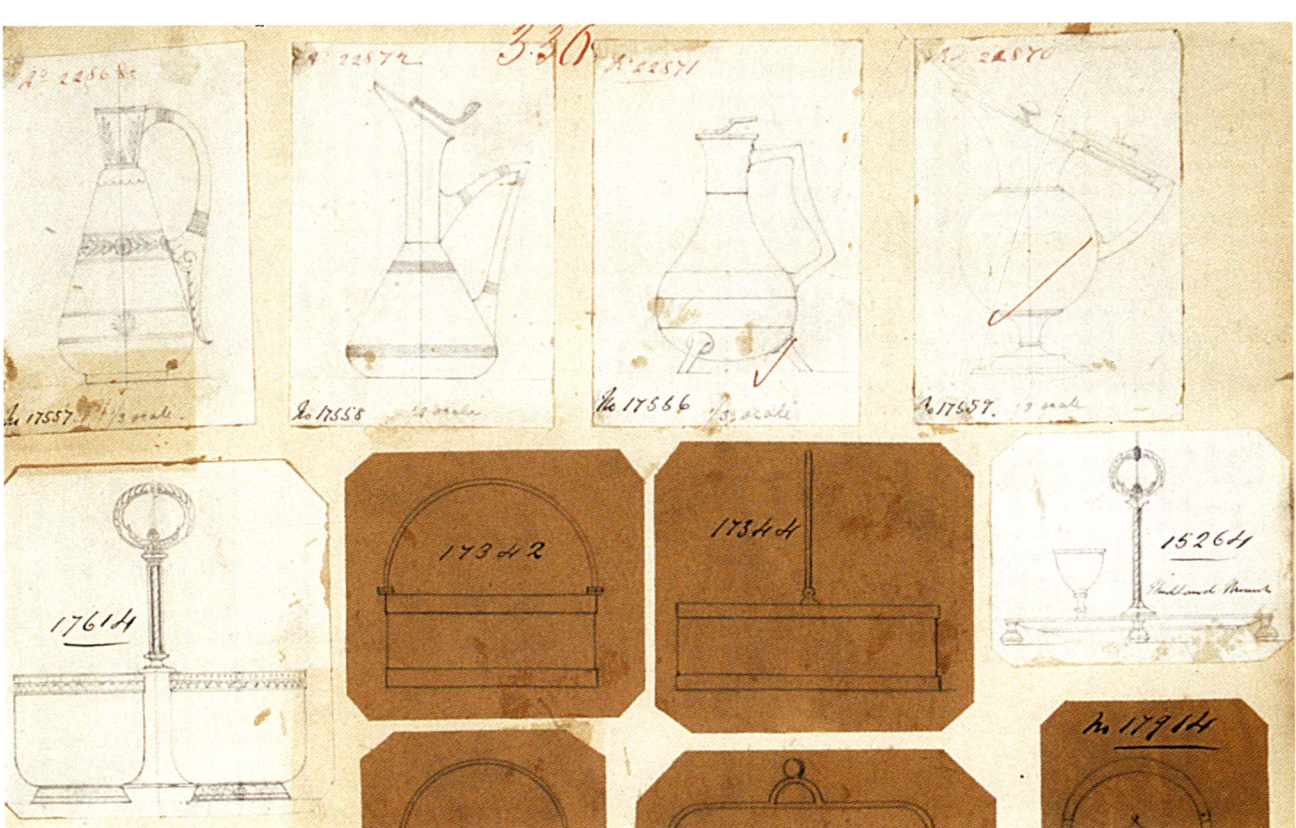

201. Silver-plate and glass cruet set, h. 17 cm, marked Elkington.

202. Silver-plate and glass cruet, h. 13 cm, marked Elkington & Co., 1885.

204. Silver-plated pitcher, h. 22 cm, marked Elkington, registered 1885.

203. Silver-plated conical bowl, h. 8 cm, marked Elkington & Co., registered 22865 for 1885.

Elkington & Co. 1865–1890

205. Silver jug, h. 17 cm, hallmark for 1885.

206. Three-piece silver-plated tea set with ebonized handles, teapot h. 16.5 cm, marked Elkington & Co., 1885.

207. Silver-plated bowl, h. 7.5 cm, marked Elkington & Co., circa 1885.

1883
Richard Perry, Son & Co., Wolverhampton

208. Brass and wood candlestick, h. 14.3 cm, marked "Dr Dresser's Design", Perry mark, registered 1883.

Little is known about Perry, Son & Co., but they were specialists in japanning. Dresser's association with them starts with a design for a candlestick, which was registered in 1883. The quality of their goods was modest, but their products perhaps come closest to Dresser's ideal of beauty in everyday objects. They are marked "Dr Dresser's Design".

Charles Holme, Dresser's old partner who became editor of *The Studio* magazine, wrote in 1898: "The strenuous efforts of Mr Dresser to raise the national level of design, not by producing costly bric-a-brac for millionaires, but by dealing with products within the reach of the middle classes, if not the masses themselves, deserve very hearty recognition".

209. Painted metal and wood candlestick, h. 10 cm, signed, marked Perry, register mark 112571, circa 1890.

210. Kettle made of copper with a *papier mâché* insulating jacket, h. 23.5 cm, marked "Dr Dresser's Design", circa 1883.

Richard Perry, Son & Co. 1883

211. Painted metal candlestick, h. 12.5 cm, signed, circa 1883.

Richard Perry, Son & Co. 1883

212. *Left to right*: candlestick in laquered metal, h. 14 cm, marked "Dr Dresser's Design", registered 1883; brass candlestick, h. 13 cm, marked "Dr Dresser's Design", circa 1883.

213. Copper and wood candlestick, h. 14 cm, marked "Dr Dresser's Design", registered 1883.

214. Painted metal and wood candlestick, h. 14.3 cm, marked "Dr Dresser's Design", Perry mark, registered 1883.

1884–1886
Old Hall, Hanley

216. Ceramic vase,
h. 34 cm, circa 1885.

Based at Hanley in Staffordshire, Old Hall Earthenware was a rejuvenation of a previously famous pottery company. Dresser appears to have designed for Old Hall between 1884 and 1886. Some of the pieces produced in this period bear a facsimile signature. Of all the companies Dresser worked for, Old Hall is perhaps the least distinguished, and it is hard to believe that Dresser was satisfied with the standard of their production.

215. Ceramic vase,
h. 34 cm, circa 1885.

Old Hall 1884–1886

217. *Left to right*: ceramic plate, 23 cm sq., signed, circa 1885; ceramic plate, 23 cm sq., circa 1885; ceramic plate, 23 cm sq., circa 1885.

218. Ceramic pitcher, circa 1885.

Old Hall 1884–1886

1890–1900
Ault, Swadlicote

219. Ceramic vase, h. 49.5 cm, signed, marked no. 247, circa 1893.

William Ault was in partnership with Henry Tooth from 1883–87, after Tooth left the Linthorpe Pottery. Ault founded his own pottery in 1887, and in 1890 he bought a number of moulds to Dresser's design from the liquidation sale of the Linthorpe Pottery. Dresser subsequently signed a contract in 1893 to supply designs to Ault, specifying that the designs should bear a facsimile of his signature. Amongst the designs to emerge from the contract are the *Goat's Head*, *Tongue* and *Face* vases.

220. *Left to right*: ceramic vase, h. 8 cm, signed, marked no. 263, circa 1893; ceramic vase, h. 26 cm, signed, marked no. 268, circa 1893; ceramic vase, h. 15.5 cm, signed, marked no. 263, circa 1893.

Ault 1890–1900

221. Ceramic vase, h. 20.8 cm, signed, circa 1893.

Ault 1890–1900

222. Ceramic *Tongue* vase, h. 32 cm, signed, marked no. 248, circa 1893.

223. Three ceramic vases, signed, circa 1893.

224. Ceramic vase, h. 21 cm, signed, circa 1890.

225. Ceramic vase, h. 24 cm, signed, circa 1890.

227. Ceramic vase, h. 22 cm, signed, circa 1893.

226. Ceramic vase, h. 13 cm, signed, marked Linthorpe HT, circa 1880.

228. Ceramic vase, h. 30 cm, signed, marked no. 310, circa 1893.

229. Ceramic "Peruvian" pitcher, h. 17 cm, signed, marked no. 288, circa 1893.

230. Ceramic vase, h. 32.2 cm, signed, marked no. 248, circa 1893.

Ault 1890–1900

231. Ceramic vase, h. 26 cm, signed, circa 1893.

232. Ceramic *Frog* vase, h. 14.5 cm, signed, circa 1893. This vase belonged to Christopher Dresser.

233. Ceramic vase,
h. 26 cm, signed, marked
no. 268, circa 1893.

234. Pair of ceramic vases, h. 33 cm, signed, circa 1893.

235. Ceramic vase, h. 15.5 cm, signed, marked no. 263, circa 1893.

237. Ceramic vase, h. 52 cm, signed, circa 1890.

236. Ceramic vase, h. 21 cm, signed, circa 1893.

1888–1900
James Couper & Sons, Glasgow

James Couper & Sons were industrial glass manufacturers from Glasgow, who introduced a new range of art glass under the trademark Clutha in 1888. The organic forms of Clutha glass derive from ancient Persian and Roman examples, thus predating Tiffany's Favrile and European art glass. The pieces designed by Dresser bear the mark "Designed by C. D.".

238. *Left to right*: glass vase, diam. 11.8 cm, signed, circa 1890; glass vase, diam. 9.5 cm, signed, circa 1890; glass vase, diam. 9 cm, signed, circa 1890.

239. *Left to right*: glass vase, h. 18 cm, signed, circa 1890; glass vase, h. 8 cm, signed, circa 1890.

240. Glass vase, h. 28 cm, signed, circa 1890.

241. Glass vase,
h. 39 cm, signed,
circa 1890.

242. *Left to right*: glass vase, h. 31 cm, signed, circa 1890; glass bowl, diam. 11.5 cm, signed, circa 1890; glass vase, h. 20.8 cm, signed, circa 1890.

243. Glass vase,
h. 35 cm, signed,
circa 1890.

244. Glass vase,
h. 33.6 cm, signed,
circa 1890.

245. *Left to right*:
glass vase, h. 26 cm,
signed, circa 1890; glass
vase, h. 22 cm, signed,
circa 1890.

246. *Left to right*:
glass vase, h. 21.5 cm,
signed, circa 1890;
glass vase, h. 20.5 cm,
signed, circa 1890;
glass vase, h. 27 cm,
signed, circa 1890;
glass vase, h. 34.5 cm,
signed, circa 1890.

247. *Left to right*: glass
vase, h. 6.5 cm, signed,
circa 1890; glass bowl,
h. 11 cm, signed,
circa 1890; glass vase,
h. 10 cm, signed,
circa 1890.

248. Glass vase,
h. 21.5 cm, signed,
circa 1890.

249. Glass vase,
h. 24 cm, signed,
circa 1890.

250. *Left to right*: glass vase, h. 10 cm, signed, circa 1890; glass vase, h. 22 cm, signed, circa 1890; glass vase, h. 9.5 cm, signed, circa 1890.

251. Glass vase, h. 20.5 cm, signed, circa 1890.

Chronology

1809
Birth of Owen Jones.
1812
Birth of Augustus Welby Northmore Pugin.
1815
The battle of Waterloo, the end of the Napoleonic wars.
1819
Birth of John Ruskin.
1825
The opening of the Stockton and Darlington Railway.
1832
Samuel Morse's telegraph.
1834
Christopher Dresser is born in Glasgow. Birth of William Morris.
1836
Contrasts: or, a parallel between the noble edifices of the fourteenth and fifteenth centuries, and similar buildings of the present day; showing the present decay of taste by A. W. N. Pugin, published by John Grant.
1837
Foundation of the Government Schools of Design, London. Victoria is crowned Queen.
1839
Louis Daguerre invents the daguerreotype. William Henry Fox Talbot invents the photographic negative.
1840
Queen Victoria marries Albert of Saxe-Coburg-Gotha.
1841
The True Principles of Pointed or Christian Architecture by A. W. N. Pugin published by John Weale.
1842–44
Al Hambra by Owen Jones published by the author.
1843
An Apology for the Revival of Christian Architecture in England by A. W. N. Pugin published by John Weale.
1844
Glossary of Ecclesiastical Ornament and Costume by A. W. N. Pugin published by Henry G. Bohn.
1845
The Condition of the Working Classes in England by Friedrich Engels published in Leipzig.
1847
Dresser enrols as a student at the Government Schools of Design, London.
1849
Floriated Ornament by A. W. N. Pugin published by Henry G. Bohn.
The Seven Lamps of Architecture by John Ruskin published.
1851
London Great Exhibition.
The Stones of Venice by John Ruskin published by George Allen.
1852
Death of A. W. N. Pugin.
1854
Christopher Dresser marries Thirza Perry.
1855
Paris International Exhibition.
1856
The Grammar of Ornament by Owen Jones published by Day and Son.
1858
The launch of Brunel's steamship, the *Great Eastern*.
1859
The Origin of the Species by Charles Darwin published by John Murray.
The Rudiments of Botany by Christopher Dresser published.
Unity in Variety by Christopher Dresser published by James S. Virtue.
Christopher Dresser is appointed a Doctor of Philosophy by Jena University.
1860
Popular Manual of Botany by Christopher Dresser published by Adam and Charles Black.
1861
Death of Prince Albert, Prince Consort of England.
1862
London International Exhibition. The Medieval Court has exhibits by William Burges, Richard Norman Shaw, J. P. Seddon, Dante Gabriele Rossetti, G. E. Street, and William Morris, all of whom are to gain great reputations in the future. The first public exhibition of Japanese art in Britain.
The first time that Dresser exhibits designs for Minton at an Internetional Exhibition.
The Art of Decorative Design by Christopher Dresser published by Day and Son.
Development of Ornamental Art in the International Exhibition by Christopher Dresser published.
1866
Hints on Household Taste by Charles Lock Eastlake published by Longmans, Green & Co.

Chronology

1867
Paris International Exhibition. Dresser exhibits ceramic designs for Wedgwood and Minton, and cast iron for Coalbrookdale.
Gothic Forms Applied to Furniture Metalwork and Decoration for Domestic Purposes by Bruce Talbert published by S. Birbeck and Bruce Talbert.

1873
Principles of Decorative Design by Christopher Dresser published by Cassell, Petter and Calpin.

1874
Death of Owen Jones.

1874–76
Studies in Design by Christopher Dresser published by Cassell, Petter and Calpin.

1876
Philadelphia Centennial Exhibition.

1877
William Watt's *Art Furniture Catalogue* showing E. W. Godwin's designs.

1878
Paris International Exhibition.

1879
Dresser and Holme is founded. Dresser is involved until 1882. Linthorpe Pottery is founded. Dresser works for Linthorpe from 1879 to 1882.
Designs for James Dixon & Sons. Dresser works for Dixons from 1879 to 1882.
Hukin and Heath Exhibition. Dresser works for Hukin and Heath from 1878 to 1881.

1880
Dresser is appointed editor of the *Furniture Gazette*.
The Art Furnishers' Alliance is founded.

1882
Japan. Its Architecture, Art and Art Manufactures by Christopher Dresser published by Longmans, Green & Co.

1883
The Art Furnishers' Alliance is liquidated. Dresser moves to Wellesley Lodge, Brunswick Road, Sutton. Chicago World Fair.

1886
Modern Ornamentation by Christopher Dresser published by the Wellesley Studio.

1889
Paris International Exhibition.

1890
William Ault buys moulds of Dresser designs at the liquidation sale of Linthorpe.

1893
Dresser signs a contract with William Ault: it stipulates that all pieces designed by him shall bear a facsimile signature.
Founding of *The Studio*, a magazine devoted to all the arts, and illustrated by photolithography.

1896
Death of William Morris.

1899
The last article on Dresser is published in *The Studio*. At this time the magazine was run by Dresser's old collaborator Charles Holme.

1900
Paris International Exhibition.
Death of John Ruskin.

1901
Death of Queen Victoria.

1904
Dresser dies while on a business trip, at Mulhouse, France.

Bibliography

Articles and Books by Christopher Dresser

"The relation of science to ornamental art", *Royal Institution Proceedings*, II, 1857, pp. 350–352.
"On a new system of nature printing", *Journal of the Society of Arts*, V, 1857, pp. 285–304.
"Botany as adapted to the Arts", *The Art Journal*, 1857, pp. 17–20, 53–54, 86–88, 109–111, 249–252, 340–342; 1858, pp. 37–39, 237–239, 293–295, 333–335, 362–364.
"Contributions to Organographic Botany, Linnean Society", Mss.5.B.230, London, 1858.
"Botany as applied to the Fine Arts and Manufactures", *Journal of the Society of Arts*, VIII, 1859–60.
The Rudiments of Botany, Structural and Physiological, London, 1859, 2nd edn 1860.
Unity in Variety as Deduced from the Vegetable Kingdom, London, 1859, 2nd edn 1860.
"On the morphological import of certain vegetable organs", *Transactions of the Edinburgh Botanical Society*, VI, 1859, pp. 321–322.
"On the stem or axis as the fundamental organ in the vegetable structure", *Transactions of the Edinburgh Botanical Society*, VI, 1860, pp. 432–434.
Popular Manual of Botany, Edinburgh, 1860.
"The art of decorative design", *The Building News*, 1861, pp. 997–998, and 1862, pp. 8–9.
"The art of decorative design", *The Builder*, 1862, pp. 185–186.
"On decorative art", *The Planet*, 1862, pp. 123–135.
The Art of Decorative Design, London, 1862.
Development of Ornamental Art in the International Exhibition, London, 1862.
"The prevailing ornament of China and Japan", *The Building News*, 1863, pp. 387–388.
"Japanese Ornamentation", *The Builder*, 1863, pp. 308–309, 364–365, 423–424. Published anonymously.
"Art foliage", *The Building News*, 1865, pp. 307–308.
"Art and industrial exhibitions", *The Building News*, 1865, p. 212.
"The Paris Exhibition 1867", *The Chromolithograph*, 23 November 1867 – 15 February 1868, pp. 12–13, 18–19, 36–37, 51, 82–83, 97–98, 112–113, 124–125, 138–139, 154–155, 167–168, 178–179.
The Decoration of Ceilings, privately printed, London, 1868.
General Principles of Art, Decorative and Pictorial, with hints on colour, its harmonies and contrasts, privately printed, London, 1868, and Pennsylvania, 1877.
"Principles of design", *The Technical Educator*, Vols I–IV, 1870–72; Vol. I, pp. 49–51, 87–90, 120–121, 151–153, 191–192, 221–223, 229–231, 277–279, 311–313, 376–378, 403–406; Vol. II, pp. 24–26, 56–58, 87–89, 119–121, 151–154, 191–192, 248–250, 280–281, 312–313, 327–329, 375–377; Vol. III, pp. 24–26, 49–50, 104–105, 145–146, 215–217, 79–82, 360–361; Vol. IV, pp. 23–25 (published in book form as *Principles of Decorative Design*, London, 1873).
"Ornamentation considered as high art", *Journal of the Society of Arts*, XIX, 1871, pp. 217–226, 352.
"Hindrances to the progress of applied art", *Journal of the Society of Arts*, XX, 1872, pp. 435–443, 513.
Principles of Decorative Design, London, 1873.
"Good taste in house furnishing", *Furniture Gazette*, 1874, pp. 10, 37–38, 61–62, 86–87.
"Eastern art and its influence on European manufacture", *Furniture Gazette*, 1874, pp. 89–90, 111–112, 136–137, 159–160, 183–184; *Journal of the Society of Arts*, XXII, 1874, pp. 211–221.
"A retrospective glance at the Vienna exhibition", *Furniture Gazette*, 1874, pp. 277–278, 304.
"The grotesque in decorative art", *Furniture Gazette*, 1874, p. 329.
"On colour", *Furniture Gazette*, 1874, pp. 352–353, 376, 539.
"The expression of Egyptian ornament", *Furniture Gazette*, 1874, p. 479.

Bibliography

"Fitness and beauty", *Furniture Gazette*, 1874, p. 484.

"The works of Owen Jones", *Furniture Gazette*, 1874, pp. 1054–1055.

"On the true principles of art as applied to the manufacture of jet ornaments", *Whitby Times*, 23 October 1874, and *Furniture Gazette*, 1874, pp. 1264–1265.

"On the production of ornament under the influence of quasi-inspiration", *Warehousemen and Drapers' Trade Journal*, 1875, p. 341.

Studies in Design, London, 1875–76.

Carpets (in the series *British Manufacturing Industries*, ed. G. Phillips Bevan), London, 1876.

"Art Industries", "Art Museums", "Art Schools", *The Penn Monthly*, 1877, pp. 21–23, 117–126, 215–220.

"Notes on four Japanese ceilings", Victoria & Albert Museum, National Art Library, Mss.86.E.E.3.(1878). Published in *The Builder*, 1878, p. 969.

"The art manufactures of Japan", *Journal of the Society of Arts*, 1878, pp. 169–178.

"Japanese woodwork", *The Builder*, 1878, p. 654.

"Works from Japan", *The Builder*, 1878, p. 696.

"Is the rage for Queen Anne over?", *The Cabinet Maker*, I, 1880, pp. 17–19.

"Art in our homes", *Furniture Gazette*, XIII, 1880, pp. 269, 287, 305, 387, 419, 435.

"The decoration of ceilings", *Furniture Gazette*, XIII, 1880, pp. 181–182.

"Propositions", *Furniture Gazette*, XIII, 1880, pp. 90–92.

Principles of Art with Preparatory Remarks upon the Objects and Practical Aims of the Art Funishers' Alliance, London, 1881.

Japan. Its Architecture, Art and Art Manufactures, London, 1882.

"Japanese art workmanship", *Furniture Gazette*, XVII, 1882, p. 264.

"Some features of Japanese architecture and ornament", *The Architect*, 1884, pp. 384–386.

"Landscape designs", *British and Colonial Manufacturer*, 1 January 1885, supplement, pp. 2–3.

"The decoration of our homes", *The Art Amateur*, New York, 1885, Vol. 13, pp. 14–16, 33, 35 and Vol. 14, pp. 110–112.

Modern Ornamentation, London, 1886.